W9-CJP-043

TEN MAKERS OF MODERN PROTESTANT THOUGHT

TEN MAKERS OF MODERN PROTESTANT THOUGHT

SCHWEITZER—RAUSCHENBUSCH—TEMPLE—
KIERKEGAARD—BARTH—BRUNNER—
NIEBUHR—TILLICH—BULTMANN—BUBER

Edited by
GEORGE L. HUNT

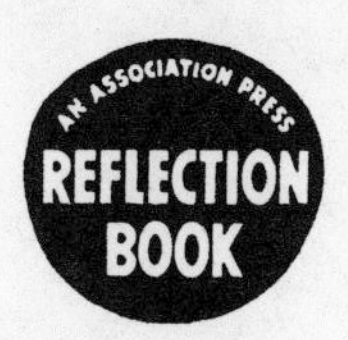

ASSOCIATION PRESS • New York

TEN MAKERS OF MODERN PROTESTANT THOUGHT

Association Press, 291 Broadway, New York 7, N. Y.

Library of Congress catalog card number: 58-6478
Printed in the United States of America

EDITOR'S DEDICATION

This book is gratefully inscribed
to
PAUL S. MINEAR
for his *Eyes of Faith*

CONTENTS

INTRODUCTION

THE MEN AND THE MOVEMENTS

BY GEORGE L. HUNT*

The person who buys this book probably does so because he has heard of some of the men in it and wants to know more about them and Protestant thought in the century in which he is living.

The reader asks himself at least three questions before he begins reading: "Why were these particular men selected as makers? What is the central element in the thought of each of them? Where does each one fit into the stream of twentieth-century Protestantism?"

The articles attempt to answer the second question, and deal primarily with the *thought* of these men

* George L. Hunt is adult editor of the Presbyterian Board of Christian Education, Philadelphia, Pa., and editor of *Crossroads,* the magazine in which six of these essays appeared originally.

rather than their life histories. The third question will be answered in the rest of this essay. At the beginning, let me reply to the first one.

The ten names selected for essays represent a personal judgment of the editor, arrived at after consultation with a number of other persons. These are the men whom I judge to be the pioneers in Protestant thought from 1900 to 1958, pioneers in the sense of opening up new trails of exploration and exerting the strongest influence on the course of Protestantism at this time.

The articles are arranged chronologically, according to the time when these men have been most prominent and influential, particularly in American Protestantism. This does not mean that they have lost their influence after their "heyday" but only that their initial impacts were made in this order. Thus, I would suggest that Schweitzer, Rauschenbusch, and Temple (and what they represent), are the chief figures of the first thirty years of this century; Kierkegaard (even though he lived a hundred years ago), Barth, Brunner, and Niebuhr flourished in the thirties and forties; and as we go into the second half of the century Tillich, Bultmann, and Buber are making the strongest impact upon Protestant thought. These are only approximate divisions, of course; and I want to reiterate that I speak of *initial* impact—most of these men have not lost their influence yet, nor are they likely to do so.

Developments in Protestant Thought Since 1900

In describing in as few words as possible the developments to which these men have made major contributions, I suggest we look at four areas of Protestant thought: Bible study, social concern, theology, and the nature and mission of the church. There is not the space here to trace the developments in these areas. What I shall do is indicate *where we stand today,* trusting that the interested reader will study one of the books listed under "For Further Reading" to learn how we got here. I shall locate the subjects of these essays in the appropriate area, although one mark of our century is the fruitful way in which these areas and the men most prominent in them have overlapped.

1. *Bible study.* The serious and careful study of the Bible today requires the use of certain principles of interpretation which are the outcome of much labor and controversy in the life of the church since 1900. These principles are also a pretty good indication of

the theological situation in Protestantism today. They are therefore worth describing in some detail.

These principles of Bible interpretation were drawn up by a study commission of the World Council of Churches in the summer of 1949, and all direct quotations in the following paragraphs are from the report of that commission. We have here an excellent illustration of the way these four areas are interrelated. It is also a sign of the century that scholars from many different Protestant traditions could meet together and agree on these basic principles of Bible study.

Behind the principles for the interpretation of a specific Bible passage are certain "theological presuppositions." Christians must listen to the Bible as God's living Word. The primary message of the Bible "concerns God's gracious and redemptive activity for the saving of sinful man that he might create in Jesus Christ a people for himself." To this message man must respond in faith and obedience. The study of the Bible is done by each Christian from within the tradition of his own particular church. But "it is agreed that the center and goal of the whole Bible is Jesus Christ." The unity of the Old and New Testament "is not to be found in any naturalistic development, or in any static identity, but in the ongoing redemptive activity of God in the history of one people, reaching its fulfillment in Christ."

The reader may wonder what is remarkable about these "presuppositions." They do not sound very different from the point of view he has always known. They are significant, however, because they affirm much that scholars of the nineteenth century ignored or denied. The scholar who holds this point of view today has come to it only after serious critical study of Scripture. He is not giving lazy acquiescence to an old faith. He is declaring what he himself has found to be true, often only after great travail.

The difference between a twentieth-century "Christological" perspective on the Bible and the same perspective held a hundred years before is that today this perspective grows out of "a historical and critical examination of the text." This includes the determination of the text itself, its language, and the accuracy of the documents available; the literary form of the passage; the historical situation surrounding the writing of the passage under study; the meaning which the words had for the original author and hearer or reader; the understanding of the passage in the light of its total context and the background out of which it emerged. Such principles as these were strongly resisted by conservatives late in the nineteenth and early in the twentieth centuries; yet today they are essential and accepted equipment for any serious study of Scripture.

In the study of an Old Testament passage, the student looks at it in relation to the revelation of God to Israel, and then in relation to the New Testament "in order to view the passage in that perspective." In the case of a New Testament passage, the student studies it in *its* setting and context, "then turns to the Old Testament to discover its background in God's former revelation. Returning again to the New Testament one is able to see and expound the passage in the light of the whole scope of the holy history which is the underlying theme of the Bible."

The report also deals with the discovery of the biblical teaching on a specific social or political issue and with the application of the biblical message to the modern world; but we have used enough of it for our purpose, which is to indicate where we stand in biblical interpretation today. The introductions and notes of the *Westminster Study Edition of the Holy Bible* and *The Interpreter's Bible* use these principles.

In this book Albert Schweitzer and Rudolf Bultmann represent the area of Bible study. They happen to stand at either end of our period also. Schweitzer's emphasis on eschatology in the teachings of Jesus, and his demonstration of the fact that we do not know enough to write a "biography" of Jesus turned New Testament study in a whole new direction. The significance of these two ideas lies in the fact that in emphasizing eschatology Schweitzer was calling for a greater fidelity to the biblical message, while in demonstrating how little we know about the historical Jesus he prepared the way for re-examination of the relation between the Christ of history and of faith.

Bultmann did pioneering work in biblical criticism in the first decades of this century; but his efforts to "demythologize" the biblical record (see the essay) is a more recent development and is just now being explored for its value in making the Bible speak to this and future generations. The names of Martin Dibelius, C. H. Dodd, W. F. Albright (the archeologist), Edgar Goodspeed, Oscar Cullman, and Walter Eichrodt should also be mentioned in this area.

2. *Social concern*. The significant development in this area is the emphasis on the *corporate* aspects of social responsibility. We have passed from conceiving of morality and ethics in individualistic terms to the point where we are now more aware that evil has social causes as well as consequences, and that the exercise of moral responsibility is the work of the

corporate community seeking to affect the power structures and patterns of society, and recognizing that it itself is affected by them. This does not mean that there is no place for individualism (freedom to be an individual is, in fact, one of the major social problems of our time). But we now realize that deeds of mercy and justice between individuals, though worth while and necessary, do little to change the society that causes injustice.

In the words of Dillenberger and Welch, this new viewpoint represents "an apparently permanent shift in the Christian attitude toward social institutions in relation to man's salvation. Earlier it had been assumed that the patterns of the social order were fixed. . . . Now, however, social institutions themselves were seen to be more malleable, and both redemptive and restrictive in relation to the spiritual life. . . . Now men felt required, as part of their Christian witness, to conceive of the transformation of the social structures as such, and of the creation of new patterns." †[1]

Though many have contributed to this development, this change is associated primarily with the names of

† Notes and documentation for all chapters will be found at the end of the book, beginning on page 123.

Walter Rauschenbusch and Reinhold Niebuhr. (See the essays.)

3. *Theology*. The movement in theology with which this part of our century will be identified is usually called "neo-orthodoxy"; but Waldo Beach's designation of "neo-Protestantism" is better. It was set in motion by Karl Barth, carried on by Emil Brunner and many others; and in America is usually associated with the name of Reinhold Niebuhr, although there are wide differences among these men and Niebuhr disclaims his own role as a theologian.

Neo-Protestantism represents a rediscovery of the vitality of Reformation theology. It has reaffirmed the sovereignty of God as One who is other than man, but who is actively involved in man's affairs and is Lord of all life. It has declared that God makes himself known in Jesus Christ his Son; and Jesus Christ (the man who is God, the God who has become man, second person of the Trinity) is known in and through the Bible. It has included a fresh appreciation of the church's teaching about the nature of man; created in the image of God, man has fallen from that estate and needs the redemption and reconciliation that only Christ can bring. Concepts like eschatology, the kingdom of God, and the church have been re-examined and revivified.

This century has seen the rise of psychiatry and psychoanalysis and of experience-centered education. These disciplines have affected the teaching and preaching of the church. But the philosophical movement closest to theology is existentialism. Kierkegaard is the "fountainhead" of this movement and he has exerted a profound influence on all the men in this book from Barth on, and on Protestant thinking in general. It is impossible to define existentialism briefly. We can only refer the reader to the essays, and particularly to the book by David E. Roberts mentioned at the end of the Kierkegaard essay.

The century has been rich in good theologians. To name a few: Nels Ferré, Anders Nygren, Gustaf Aulen, John and Donald Baillie.

4. *The nature and mission of the church.* Two closely related developments have taken place in this area. This has been the century of the "ecumenical church"; activities of church co-operation have abounded, and the union of denominations has taken place. We need only mention the formation of the International Missionary Council, the National Council of the Churches of Christ in America, the World Council of Churches, and the World Council of Christian Education—all

formed in this century—to make this point clear. The line between "sending" churches and "receiving" churches in the mission field is rapidly breaking down, and "one church" is nearer to reality than it has ever been before. William Temple was one of the leaders of this movement (though the essay deals with a different facet of his witness). To his name should be added the names of John R. Mott, John A. Mackay, Bishop Brent, and many other leaders of the modern missionary movement.

The other development has been an increased concern about the nature of the church. This has grown directly out of the ecumenical movement. What is the church? What is its place in the plan of God? What is the meaning of the sacraments? of church orders and organizations and ministries? What is the mission of the church in our kind of world? These are live and important questions which will occupy a prominent place in Protestant life and thought in the years ahead.

Meanwhile, as in every age, the church faces what is today called "the problem of communication." How can the ancient gospel be made alive and meaningful to this age of "anxiety" and "scientism?" Tillich and Bultmann are intensely concerned with this matter, and regard their work as laying the groundwork for intelligent communication about the faith. It seems also that the Jewish philosopher Martin Buber has something to say to Protestants on this same score, with his stress on the importance of the personal in human relationships. Certainly no emphasis is more needed in our kind of world than this.

FOR FURTHER READING

John Dillenberger and Claude Welch, *Protestant Christianity* (New York: Charles Scribner's Sons, 1954).
Arnold S. Nash, ed., *Protestant Thought in the Twentieth Century* (New York: The Macmillan Company, 1951).

I

ALBERT SCHWEITZER

BY HENRY A. RODGERS*

Enthusiastic admirers have called Albert Schweitzer the "greatest man in the world." Whether or not he deserves this superlative title, there is no doubt about the impact made by the force of his personality upon the world of our day.

Born in 1875, he grew up in the little town of Günsbach in the then German, now French province of Alsace. His father was pastor of the Evangelical congregation. At the age of thirty Albert Schweitzer resolved to give his life to some task of service to humanity as an expression of his stewardship to Christ. After considering various projects, he found his call in an advertisement of the Paris Missionary Society for a medical doctor to serve in French Equatorial

* Henry A. Rodgers is professor of Greek and Bible at Grove City College, Grove City, Pa.

Africa. He had already earned doctorates in philosophy, theology, and music. To these he now added a fourth in medicine. Then he offered his services to the Paris Society.

Schweitzer held some theological views which were unpopular at the time. Because of this, the Society nearly turned him down, and finally accepted him only on condition that he would not preach. In 1913, with his wife, a nurse, he set out for Africa. At Lambaréné he built a hospital from the ground up. By 1914 he had more practice than he could handle. For over forty years he has given himself in this work as a true and loyal servant of Jesus Christ.

Reaction to Liberalism

In this chapter on Albert Schweitzer we are primarily interested in his contribution to religious thought, and must therefore bypass the fascinating story of his medical work in Africa.

He is primarily a New Testament scholar; and his major work in New Testament study was a reaction against the liberal school of German theology of his day. The principal goal of these liberals was to study Jesus with modern methods, and so make him intelligible to the modern mind. They tried to rediscover "the historical Jesus" as a man who had lived in a certain period of history, under certain political and social conditions, and had proclaimed his universal message. Above all, they wanted to be strictly scientific, by which they meant eliminating everything that might be attributed to superstition, like the miracles, or Jesus' supernatural relationship with God. Such things, they explained, belonged to the thinking of those who wrote down Jesus' teachings in the Gospels, and not to Jesus himself. Jesus was thought of as the great Teacher, and the "kingdom of God" would come when all men fully understood and obeyed his teachings.

Among the "superstitious" parts of the New Testament that the liberals rejected were the many references to the Second Coming of Christ, the Last Judgment, the end of the world, heaven, and hell. These are known to theologians as eschatology, the doctrine of the Last Things. That these loom large in the Gospel records, and even in the recorded sayings of Jesus, no one has ever doubted. But Schweitzer became convinced that they should not be eliminated from the teachings of Jesus—on the contrary, Jesus as a man who had lived in the generation that believed in these things had actually believed in them himself.

In his book *The Mystery of the Kingdom of God,*

Schweitzer deals with three mysteries, which he believes were in the mind of Jesus and which seem to explain all the eschatological sayings of Jesus. The first, the mystery of the kingdom of God, Schweitzer finds in Matthew 10:23 where Jesus tells the twelve apostles, as he sends them out to preach, "Verily I say unto you, ye shall not have gone over the cities of Israel, till the Son of man be come." [1] From this and other passages, Schweitzer decided that Jesus actually expected the Kingdom to appear in a supernatural way at that particular time, and that he was disappointed when it failed.

The second, the mystery of the Messiahship, is based on the coincidence of the phrase "who is to come" in Matthew 11:3 and 14. From this Schweitzer concluded that people thought of Jesus—not of John the Baptist—as Elijah, who was to prepare the way for the coming of Christ. Only Jesus, he insists, at that time realized that when the Son of Man should come on the clouds of heaven, it would be himself.

The third mystery, that of the Passion, is, according to Schweitzer, the most important of all. Having been disappointed about the coming of the Son of Man, that is, himself, at the time he sent out the Twelve, Jesus came to the conclusion, from Isaiah 53, that as Messiah he must first die for his people. So he foretold his death, then deliberately went to Jerusalem and provoked the authorities to crucify him, expecting in that way to bring about his own Second Coming and the kingdom of God.

Facing Fresh Questions

Schweitzer believed that he had solved the difficulties he had found in the liberal interpretation of the historical Jesus. But his solution raises as many problems as it solves. One of these is the purpose of Jesus' teachings. If he was primarily concerned with establishing a supernatural, perfect Kingdom, why should he bother to give ethical instructions like the Sermon on the Mount? Schweitzer recognized this problem and gave his answer: Such teachings were intended to show his immediate followers what they could do as works of repentance in order that the Kingdom might come. They would not be needed after the Kingdom had come, for then sin would be done away with, and those who shared in the Kingdom would naturally do the right thing. In this sense, he calls the teachings of Jesus "interim ethics," for the time being, until the Kingdom should come. (Of course, since the Kingdom has not yet come in the eschatological sense, they are still valid today.) For to Schweitzer, Jesus was not primarily a Teacher, but a Redeemer, the Christ who will be king.

This insight also answers another problem raised by Schweitzer's interpretation: that of Jesus' alleged mistakes. In connection with the mystery of the kingdom of God, Schweitzer believes that Jesus had expected the Kingdom to come at the time he sent out the twelve apostles to preach and had been disappointed and upset at its failure to materialize. Then he had come to the conclusion that he must force it to come by dying to redeem his people. This was the mystery of the Passion. If Schweitzer is right, Jesus was mistaken on both counts. The Kingdom did not appear when the twelve went out to preach, and it did not come immediately following his death. And if Jesus was mistaken about two of the "mysteries," how can we be sure he was not mistaken about the third, that of his Messiahship, that is, his certainty that he himself would be revealed as the Christ when the Kingdom should come?

Schweitzer does not answer this question in just this form, but he does deal with the basic problem in the concluding chapter of *The Quest of the Historical Jesus.*[2] To those who would claim that he has destroyed faith in Jesus, he replies that the Jesus he destroyed never really existed except in the inventive minds of the liberal theologians. He claims to have loosed Jesus from the fetters of this false interpretation and restored him to his rightful place as the great King. He even quotes with approval Paul's dictum in II Corinthians, 5:16: "Though we have known Christ after the flesh, yet now henceforth we know him no more." [3] That is, his faith is not in Jesus the man, understood in human terms, but in Christ the Son of God, whom we know by his spirit in our hearts, and to whom our response must be not in our minds, but in our wills, as we obey him.

Schweitzer was well aware that some of the liberal theologians would refuse to accept his eschatological interpretations of Jesus. He made them come to grips with the problem, however, and so he was partially responsible for the method of Bible study called "Form Criticism." These scholars who questioned whether Jesus had eschatological ideas were forced to attribute more and more of his sayings to the writers of the Gospels, or to the tradition from which they got their information. This in turn led to the study of the tradition itself, and became what is known as Form Criticism. This movement has produced some very learned works by such scholars as Martin Dibelius, Rudolf Bultmann, and others.

Today, largely because of Schweitzer's pioneering work, no reputable theologian can ignore the eschatological element in the Gospels. C. H. Dodd, of Cambridge, has interpreted this teaching as what he calls "realized eschatology." He points out that Jesus spoke of the Kingdom as not always future, but in some sense present. "The kingdom of God is in the midst of you." [4] Dodd therefore seeks to show that Jesus used eschatological language because it was the natural mode of expression in his day, but that he meant by it something much more universal than his contemporaries understood.

Basis for Humanitarian Work

Thus Schweitzer has affected modern Protestant thought. But he will be remembered rather as the great humanitarian, who gave up theology and philosophy to demonstrate the love of God by his medical mission to the neglected Negroes of Africa. In the last analysis, this is simply the practical expression of his faith.

It arises first from his sense of dedicated stewardship. In his *Memoirs of Childhood and Youth,*[5] he recalls winning a schoolboy fight, only to have the elation of victory snatched away by the loser's remark,

"If I had broth every day as you do, I could beat you." From that day on, Schweitzer has always believed that God gave him exceptional powers of body and mind for some special service to mankind. He is trying to perform that service at Lambaréné.

It arises also from the cardinal principle of his *Philosophy of Civilization,*[6] which is "Reverence for Life." His critics have charged that his reverence for all forms of animal life, even insects, is based on Hindu pantheism. The resemblance is coincidental. To Schweitzer, needlessly to kill another living creature, which wills to live as he wills to live, is to transgress the purpose of God in creating it. It is therefore a Christian motive.

But his devotion to his work is, more than all else, simply the expression of his obedience to the royal Christ, to whom he has unconditionally surrendered his will. As he says in the closing chapter of *The Quest of the Historical Jesus,* faith is a matter of the will, more than of the understanding. This is the basic faith by which he lives; and it is capable of commanding a devotion and self-sacrifice such as the "historical Jesus" could not call forth. On this faith let Albert Schweitzer be judged. As his Master said, "You shall know them by their fruits."

FOR FURTHER READING

Albert Schweitzer, *Out of My Life and Thought* (New York: Henry Holt and Company, Incorporated, 1949; also, New American Library, paperback edition). An autobiography.

——, *The Quest of the Historical Jesus* (New York: The Macmillan Company, 1948).

——, *The Mystery of the Kingdom of God* (New York: The Macmillan Company, 1950).

II

WALTER RAUSCHENBUSCH

BY ROBERT T. HANDY*

For about a decade, Walter Rauschenbusch was one of the best-known ministers in America. He became a national figure suddenly and unexpectedly in 1907. From then until his death in 1918, Rauschenbusch was greatly in demand as preacher, lecturer, and writer. Five important books and a number of smaller pieces came from his pen in those years. He was regarded as the central figure in the movement known as the "social gospel," which was then very influential in American Protestantism. Henry Van Dusen has classed him with Jonathan Edwards and Horace Bushnell as one of the three most influential men in the thought of the American church.

Walter Rauschenbusch was born in 1861 in Roches-

* Robert T. Handy is associate professor of church history at Union Theological Seminary, New York, N. Y.

ter, New York. His German-born father came to this country as a missionary in the middle of the last century, and soon thereafter left Lutheranism to enter the Baptist fold. Young Walter was educated in both Germany and America, and graduated from the Rochester Theological Seminary in 1886. He desired "to preach and save souls." In order to do this, he felt he must live literally by the teachings and spirit of Jesus.

It was with this spirit of commitment that he accepted the pastorate of the Second German Baptist Church in New York's tough west side, not far from the region popularly known as "Hell's Kitchen." His was a congregation of working people, and the earnest young pastor soon became acutely aware of their difficult struggles against poverty and disease, especially in hard times. Their suffering forced him to confront social problems. As he put it, his social view "did not come from the church. It came from outside. It came through personal contact with poverty, and when I saw how men toiled all their life long, hard, toilsome lives, and at the end had almost nothing to show for it; how strong men begged for work and could not get it in hard times; how little children died—oh, the children's funerals! they gripped my heart—that was one of the things I always went away thinking about—why did the children have to die?" (From an address in 1913.) Actually he suffered with his people—leaving his bed too early after an influenza attack in order to minister to sick and needy parishioners, the illness recurred and left him quite deaf. But this did not hinder his desire to improve social conditions.

Committed Christian that he was, he could not long keep his social thinking separate from his religious thinking; and so he sought to bring the two together. He read widely in social and economic literature, but also in the writings of men who were advocating concern for social issues from a distinctively Christian point of view. This was the distinctive thing about him—the effort to emphasize both evangelical faith and social reconstruction. It was then an unfamiliar combination.

A recent thoughtful analysis of Rauschenbusch by Winthrop S. Hudson is aptly entitled "A Lonely Prophet." He was lonely not only because his deafness served to isolate him somewhat from those around him but also because this fundamental aim—to combine the *religious* and the *social* passion—was so often misunderstood. Some could not believe he had the first because he had the second also; others seized upon the second but remained oblivious to the first. Yet the key to understanding him is to see that his lifework was precisely the effort to keep both emphases, with priority always on the first.

His Understanding of the Kingdom of God

The seminary from which he had graduated had not forgotten its able son, and in 1897 Rauschenbusch returned to Rochester to teach, finally settling into the chair of church history. But it was to be not as a church historian but as a social prophet that Rauschenbusch became famous. He wrote a book to discharge a debt to his former parishioners, to help ease the pressure that bore them down. *Christianity and the Social Crisis* appeared in that year of financial panic, 1907.

His thesis was that "the essential purpose of Christianity was to transform human society into the kingdom of God by regenerating all human relations and reconstituting them in accordance with the will of God," but that this purpose had been obscured through the centuries and now had to be recovered. Coming at a time when the social questions were among the most popular issues of the day, the book won instant acclaim and set its author at the forefront of the growing number of pastors and laymen anxious to deal with social concerns from a Christian viewpoint. Rauschenbusch became the leader of the social gospel movement, a career interrupted by his death of cancer in 1918.

Rauschenbusch was especially concerned to elaborate on the full meaning of the kingdom of God, and he kept both his tongue and pen busy at this task throughout his lifetime. He wrote: *Prayers of the Social Awakening* (1910), *Christianizing the Social Order* (1912), *The Social Principles of Jesus* (1916), and *A Theology for the Social Gospel* (1917).

The concept of the kingdom of God was for him a profoundly religious concept which was central in the teachings of Jesus and which included the entire life of man and society. As he said in the concluding chapter of the book that deals most with social and economic problems:

"This is a religious book from beginning to end. Its sole concern is for the kingdom of God and the salvation of men. But the kingdom of God includes the economic life; for it means the progressive transformation of all human affairs by the thought and spirit of Christ." [1]

He warned against substituting social activities for religious; he insisted that not less religion but more—of the right kind—was needed.

For Rauschenbusch, the kingdom of God was not an earthly utopia that men could create. He emphasized that it was divine in its origin, progress, and consummation. It was for him the revelation of the power, the righteousness, and the love of God. He knew it as both a present reality among men and a future hope to be fully disclosed only in the fullness of time. He did believe that it was progressively being realized:

"A progressive Kingdom of righteousness happens all the time in installments, like our own sanctification. Our race will come to an end in due time; the astronomical clock is already ticking which will ring in the end. Meanwhile we are on the march toward the kingdom of God, and getting our reward by every fractional realization of it which makes us hungry for more." [2]

He summoned men and women to serve the Kingdom in their lives:

"Every human life is so placed that it can share with God in the creation of the Kingdom, or can resist and retard its progress. The Kingdom is for each of us the supreme task and the supreme gift of God. By accepting it as a task, we experience it as a gift. By laboring for it we enter into the joy and peace of the Kingdom as our divine fatherland and habitation." [3]

The lives of many Christians were shaped by their response to the call to serve in the Kingdom task.

His Contribution

As the man who was the most conspicuous representative of the social gospel, Walter Rauschenbusch made an important and permanent contribution to American Christian thought. He and those like him pointed out in an unforgettable way the social dimension of life and the social aspects of the gospel of Christ.

To be sure, he was the child of his time, and most of us would find ourselves quite out of sympathy with some of his statements. In explaining what Jesus' idea of the Kingdom was, he no doubt read in too much of his own progressive and evolutionary view, and did not give proper weight to the eschatological aspect. Strong for the Kingdom, he probably did not value highly enough the role of the church. In stressing the immanence of God, in identifying him so closely with humanity, Rauschenbusch minimized the transcendence, the majesty, and the sovereignty of God. In defining sin as essentially selfishness he did less than justice to the classic Christian understanding of sin as pride. As for his social views, a case can be made that they lacked the sturdy quality and real insight of his religious thought. They reflected the mild progressive radicalism of the type that had considerable vogue before World War I; though he was not a socialist, his analysis of the social order drew on socialist thought. And clearly he overestimated the degree to which the nation and its institutions had become Christianized.

His contribution, therefore, was set in a framework that clearly bears the stamp of an age that has passed. Yet it is impressive to observe how he avoided the pitfalls into which the later social gospel slipped. Though he was influenced by the optimism of his time, he also understood the tragic character of life and warned that men and nations might take the wrong road. Although some of his followers in their social passion neglected personal religion, Rauschenbusch himself never did and, had his followers listened to his full message, they would not have neglected it either. He never confused social reconstruction, necessary as he believed it to be, with the experience of salvation, which he sought to enrich and expand by bringing it into proper relation to the kingdom of God.

FOR FURTHER READING

D. R. Sharpe, *Walter Rauschenbusch* (New York: The Macmillan Company, 1942.) A book about Rauschenbusch, now out of print. Available in libraries.

Benjamin E. Mays, ed., *A Gospel for the Social Awakening: Selections from the Writings of Walter Rauschenbusch* (New York: Association Press, 1950).

Benson Y. Landis, ed., *A Rauschenbusch Reader* (New York: Harper & Brothers, 1957).

III

WILLIAM TEMPLE

BY C. EDWARD HOPKIN*

An Archbishop of Canterbury, whose father had also held that office, might be expected to contribute only nineteenth-century ideas to twentieth-century thought. William Temple, however, brought his religious heritage to bear upon current problems, especially in the tortured fields of theology, social ethics, and ecumenicity. In point of time he was born in 1881 and died in 1944, his mature activity spanned the two world wars. In point of quality, he was a speculative philosopher with orthodox beliefs, an aristocrat with a strong social conscience and a believer in apostolic succession who participated actively in the ecumenical movement. Though he was outstanding in

* C. Edward Hopkin is Holy Trinity professor of systematic theology and ethics at the Divinity School of the Protestant Episcopal Church in Philadelphia, Pa.

all three areas—philosophy, social needs, and the ecumenical movement—we shall in this essay deal mainly with his philosophic contribution to theology.

Thirty Years Ago

In order to assess Temple's contribution to the field of theology, it is necessary to go behind the excitements of the movements which are today in the foreground, and to recall the religious situation of the first two decades of this century. The question then was, "What can an educated man believe?" Every Protestant churchman who is old enough can recall for himself how his church met, or attempted to meet, this problem. Science, as popularly understood, had reduced all reality to matter, and all event to predictable consequence from material causes. Man was merely one of the consequences. To make matters worse, scientific exuberance was wedded to philosophical naïveté. Those of us who lived through that time were only dimly aware that this simple picture of a wholly material reality answered some questions at the price of raising others which it could not answer. An occasional scientist publicly gave science's blessing to a certain kind of religious belief, or an occasional preacher gave religion's blessing to science, but this was a soothing ointment. It did not cure.

Some accepted the incompatibility of religious belief with scientific determinism, and declared that one side or the other had all the truth. Others attempted a compromise by stripping religion of miracle. In thus denying freedom to God, these persons attributed a great deal of freedom to man. Still others experimented or dogmatized in other ways, seeking to make peace or draw sharp lines in the relation of science and religion.

Like all other Churches, the Church of England first came to grips with scientism, not in the field of scientific determinism but in the field of the scientific dissection and criticism of the documents of the Bible. However, unlike most other Churches, the Church of England was not in an unresolved either-or situation with respect to this problem when Temple began his adult activities. A respectable group of scholars and theologians, under the leadership of Charles Gore, had already combined the acceptance of scientific biblical criticism with orthodoxy of belief. Opinions differed, and many still differ, on how successfully they achieved this combination. Nevertheless, they had proclaimed their stand on this ground by the publication, in 1890, of a widely read series of essays, under the unifying title *Lux Mundi*. "Christ, the Light of the

World," was the banner under which a world view could be proclaimed which would allow for a scientifically amenable nature on the one hand, and a personalist view of God and man on the other. Yet the emphasis was still placed upon the Bible as revelation and as properly subject, at the same time, to scientific investigation and analysis. The field was open for a competent Anglican, working in the same milieu, to develop this world view with sufficient thoroughness to meet the broader philosophic problems raised by scientific materialism and determinism.

William Temple was equipped for the task in a host of ways. A flair for the Greek language; sound training in Platonism; a vigorous mind and body; a firsthand, natural acquaintance with the best thought of his time in England and Germany; and an almost unlimited opportunity to develop this equipment without hindrance—these ingredients are easily seen in his early life. Born in 1881, while his father was Bishop of Exeter, his formal education was obtained at Rugby and Oxford, with approximately a year at the University of Jena. It is hardly to the point here to follow his career as Headmaster of Repton (1910), Rector of St. James', Piccadilly (1914), Canon of Westminster (1919), Bishop of Manchester (1921), and Archbishop of Canterbury (1942). The thread we rather wish to follow is that of this philosophical approach to the Christian Faith.

Temple's Philosophical Approach

He did approach the Christian Faith. He did not merely accept it as packaged by his background. Intensely interested in religion and in Christianity as an experience of God, he had by no means an easy time with all its doctrines as defined by the Church of England. From two to three years of serious correspondence with his bishop preceded his entrance into Holy Orders in 1908. At this time he was a Fellow of Queens College, Oxford, lecturing on Plato.

In 1909 he was invited to deliver a series of lectures to the Student Christian Movement in London. These lectures he later expanded and published under the title, *The Faith and Modern Thought.* In these lectures he develops the theme that religious experience is a given thing, like the experiences upon which science builds, and that although the classical arguments for the existence of God do not really reach their goal, the approach from experience can be shown to parallel, in many ways, the approach to truth enjoyed by the scientific method and to deserve a similar respect. Furthermore, both the scientific method and that of religious experience seem at one in crying out for a view of reality containing Will and Purpose. This may, he continues, look like a mere variant of the futile arguments of the philosophers, but it can be shown that the religion of the Bible is not a philosophical argument at all. It is a declaration of experience which speaks with authority.

Nevertheless, the futility of the philosophical effort to prove God should not be taken to mean that the person who believes on the basis of experience cannot state his belief in philosophical terms, in accordance with the criteria established by the soundest thought of his own day. Now, for an educated Englishman of the first third of the twentieth century, the soundest thought available was some form of Platonism, in which Idea and Mind are terms indicative of a prior reality giving origin and meaning to all materialized particulars. Developing this classic theme as a believer, Temple made two excursions into the deeps of philosophy in the books *Mens Creatrix* (1917) and *Christus Veritas* (1924). Here we encounter the claim that in the doctrine of the Incarnation the Christian has a foundation for a metaphysical understanding of the universe which can be explicated much further than Anglican theology had so far attempted to do. Value is seen to be the clue to existence, rather than existence the clue to value. In this sense Christ is "the truth" in the philosophical realm as well as in the religious realm. Philosophy and religion thus find, for the believer, their unity in Christ, in whom the believer sees consequently his own integration of intellect and faith.

Something, however, is left out of the intellectual effort thus far. That something is the proper relating of this Christianized Platonic metaphysic with the concern for the event itself, which historic Christianity and science share with one another. In other words, it is one thing to look at reality in the quasi-divine manner, as in the prologue to the Fourth Gospel, and it is something else again to look at the world through the events of the world.

The opportunity to present this view from the ground up was given to William Temple, then Archbishop of York, when he was invited to deliver the Gifford Lectures in the University of Glasgow for two successive years, beginning in 1932. These are published under the title, *Nature, Man and God.*[1]

The Gifford Lectures

One of the conditions imposed upon the Gifford lecturers is that they confine themselves to the field of natural religion. The standpoint and methods of revealed theology must, for this purpose, be renounced. Perhaps it was due to this restriction, or to his greater maturity, that Dr. Temple paid better attention to method in these lectures. In any event, *Nature, Man and God* is a much more carefully prepared work than were his earlier philosophic constructions. The author is less exuberant, more painstaking. The impression is left of a conscientious examining of the problems of theism. Criteria are more seriously observed and results are more cautiously marshaled.

Never one to avoid an issue, Dr. Temple accepts the full implications of contemporary science, logic, and philosophy as he understands them. Then he moves on to the restatement and evaluation for theism of such difficult matters as freedom and determinism; transcendence and immanence; religious authority and freedom; the problem of evil, grace, and human freedom; the concept of eternal life, its relation to value and to the meaning of history; and, finally, the unsatisfied status of natural religion which creates more demands than it alone can meet.

The book is not easy reading. Furthermore, it came too late to be considered publicly as an answering of religion's worst problems, because by that time the banners of neo-orthodoxy were drawing the attention of the reading public away from such laborious efforts of the human reason. Yet, in spite of these handicaps, *Nature, Man and God* did something to twentieth-century religious thought beyond the confines of Anglicanism. An archbishop had shown that he could be an amateur in philosophy in the best sense of the word "amateur." With all the error which specialists might find in some of his expressions, at least he could not be accused of avoiding either their language or their problems.

More Than a Philosopher

His influence was further enhanced by the fact that he also refused to be a typical professional in religion. Ever since his student days he had leaned to the left, not only in his social thinking but in his organized activity. The frontier of social ethics brought him into continual, active association with workingmen's organizations. His participation in interchurch relations was pointed up by his chairmanship of the Edinburgh Conference on Faith and Order in 1937. These are but the slightest indications of a life of intense activity for human welfare and fellowship which, for him, were commanded by his religious beliefs. He demonstrated amply that for the man of genuine faith, thought leads to action, and loyalty to co-operation and fellowship.

The twentieth century was nearly half spent when Archbishop Temple died on September 26, 1944. Not many men in such high position have been so free from the technique of escape; or, to put it positively, have been so ready to accept and answer the hardest questions of the times.

FOR FURTHER READING

F. A. Iremonger, *William Temple, Archbishop of Canterbury: His Life and Letters* (London: Oxford University Press, 1948).

William Temple, *Christianity and Social Order* (New York: The Macmillan Company, 1952).

A. E. Baker, ed., *William Temple's Teaching* (Philadelphia: Westminster Press, 1951). Out of print.

IV

SOREN KIERKEGAARD

BY FRED J. DENBEAUX*

Sören Kierkegaard would not be comfortable with the nervously cautious thinkers of our age. He not only was indifferent to public opinion but he attacked all those who relied upon the support of the masses. For Kierkegaard, the truth, the costly and painful truth, constitutes the only standard of the right. The question of truth before every man is the question of whether he will dare to pay the cost.

Kierkegaard was born in Denmark in 1813 and, except for a few brief visits to Berlin, lived out his life in his homeland. He was very close to his father who, in spite of the fact that he was a practical man, communicated to his son a deeply serious concern for the problems of Christian life and thought. After the completion of his work at the university and after some years of indecision, Kierkegaard began to prepare himself for a church parish. Because of a number of factors, not the least of which was his need for per-

* Fred J. Denbeaux is chairman of the Bible department at Wellesley College, Wellesley, Mass., and a Presbyterian minister.

sonal freedom, he was unable to become a clergyman. Similarly he fell in love and planned for marriage, but for many reasons, including that of temperament, he was unable to marry. Occupied with neither a vocation nor a family and supported by a fairly substantial inheritance from his father, he was able to produce an incredibly large amount of literature. For this we have reason to be grateful, since his thinking has added a measure of depth to the thought of many contemporary Protestants, Jews, and Roman Catholics.

The Creature Thinking About God

Let us examine the thought of this man who has come to be one of the major influences on Protestant theology in this century.

Kierkegaard has no interest in the traditional arguments for the existence of God. Whatever is ultimate and meaningful can never be proved. God is never an object, not even a divine object. He is either the Absolute, by which *we* are proved, or he is nothing.

In either case, God is not contained within our system of logic. Thus, in a very important passage, Kierkegaard says, "So also with the proof for God's existence. As long as I keep my hold on the proof, i.e., continue to demonstrate, the existence does not come out, if for no other reason than that I am engaged in proving it; but when I let the proof go, the existence is there." Here Kierkegaard reflects the biblical notion that *faithful obedience* rather than thought describes man's relationship to God. Whenever I try to prove that God exists, I actually lose my relationship to him, since proving moves me from the role of a servant to that of a lawyer.

Kierkegaard also believes that we cannot come to God through thought because we can never leave the *structure* in which we exist as *creatures*. Any thought about God always, if it be true thought, carries with it the understanding of both the relationship between God and man and the difference between the Creator and the creature. Kierkegaard says that God is "the limit to which the reason repeatedly comes." Thus one of the surest indications that there is a God is found in the fact that we have difficulty "thinking" God. Our mind cannot produce the images that will sustain a true knowledge of God. We can produce as many arguments for him as against him. Thinking cannot produce . . . God. Our mind is shattered by God in the sense that one must say that he believes in God not because his mind has found God but because it has failed to find him. Only as one is sensitive to the *limit* can one be sure that one is responding as a creature must to his Creator.

Thus Kierkegaard reintroduces the biblical and Reformed notion that we shall think about God as a creature or we shall not think about him at all.

How Can We Understand Christ?

We can best understand Kierkegaard's contribution if we remember that he defended the orthodox view of Jesus in quite unorthodox language. He accepted the traditional and trinitarian view of Jesus Christ. What he was trying to do was to create a new approach to our ancient faith.

Again, as Kierkegaard sees it, our approach to Jesus Christ is through a *relationship* and not through speculation. This means that Christ is not a problem in doctrine. One cannot get to Christ through correct thinking. Christ is understood only through his Lordship over our lives. Or, to put it the other way around, we can understand Christ, not through ideas, but through discipleship.

We begin, then, by understanding that Christ is Lord, not because of what he teaches but because of what he does. He brings to men not only the assurance of God's love but also the possibility of being participants in that love, through receiving the grace of God's forgiveness. All of Kierkegaard's art, at this point, is calculated to evoke a response from his readers. He does not so much instruct us on his view of Christ as he tries to have us respond and, out of our response, to understand. This means that we must, as we think through the whole problem of Jesus Christ, be sure that we do not get lost in the externals of discussion. Christ is not Lord to us because of the authority of the church or because he did miracles in an astounding and interesting manner. He is our Lord because we are his disciples or he is not Lord at all.

A characteristic phrase of Kierkegaard's is "the solitary individual." No one has stressed the importance of individual decision (and of individuality) more than he, for we do not become disciples in a crowd. We become disciples only as individuals. We become disciples not because others have believed but in spite of it. We become disciples of Christ not because the world supports us, but because it does not. Every Christian must first approach Christ in this manner, without proof, without support, and in utter faith.

The Offense of Faith

Faith, however, is not easy. It is certainly not an act of blindness, for God in his wisdom makes it impossible to accept Christ easily. Kierkegaard points out over and over again that Christ comes to us in a form that insults both our notion of self-reliance and our intelligence. He makes much of the saying of Jesus, "Blessed is he who takes no offense at me." It is inevitable either that we shall be offended or that we shall believe.

What is the offense of faith? It can take many forms. We would welcome a God of light, but he comes to us crucified. We would welcome a God with whom we could be happy, and instead we are confronted with him whom we have slain. We are offended because we can never come before God neutrally but always in guilt. We are offended because the Christ who comes does not come in the form that we expect. We would be happier if he came as a god of war, so that we could join our sword to his in the battle against unrighteousness (always conveniently with the enemy and never with ourselves.) But the Christ does not come with a sword, and he asks us to put our sword away; so we are offended.

Therefore, Christ is always the occasion of either offense or faith. He is the one either before whom we stumble and fall on our knees or else from whom we turn in defensive pride. He is our Saviour, but we shall never know him as such if we become offended, because it is from ourselves that he saves us.

What makes man human? Although Kierkegaard does not emphasize the word, he thinks of man in terms of his *creatureliness.*

Man's creatureliness lies in the fact that he stands between life and death. Made in the image of God, he knows what it means to feel the presence of eternity. Feeling the nearness of eternity, utterly dependent upon it for his meaning, he also knows that he dies, and that he cannot escape death. These two factors constitute both his problem and his possibility of for immortaliy, creates his anguish or his *nervous humanness.*

Man sins in that he is unwilling to live in faith and therefore to be nervously human. He prefers to live either with life or with death but not with both. He seeks to escape creatureliness either by pretending that he will not die or by assuming that there is no eternity.

He refuses to bear uncertainty and anguish. Either he turns his back on death by pretending that immortality is automatically a part of all life or he tries to forget his anguish by becoming an animal.

It is precisely this anguish, this willingness to live neither as an animal (unaware of eternity) nor as an angel (indifferent to death), which marks the humanness from which we fall when we sin. It is also this greatness. Knowing mortality, even while he hungers humanness, this willingness to risk death as we trust God, which signals the beginning of our redemption. Thus the Christ of love returns us to our creatureliness by saving us from the need of false securities. The Lord Christ, by accepting death even while he trusted in God, restores meaning to creaturely existence. By faith man dares to become what without faith he was afraid to be—a human being.

FOR FURTHER READING

Sören Kierkegaard, *Purity of Heart* (New York: Harper & Brothers, 1956). Introduction by Douglas V. Steere. This is the best book to begin with for an understanding of Kierkegaard's philosophy.

Robert Bretall, ed., *A Kierkegaard Anthology* (Princeton, N. J.: Princeton University Press, 1946). Read selections in this book, then decide where you want to go next.

David E. Roberts, *Existentialism and Religious Belief* (New York: Oxford University Press, 1957). Read this book for an introduction and understanding of existentialism. It contains a good section on Kierkegaard.

V

KARL BARTH

BY THOMAS F. TORRANCE*

Karl Barth is incontestably the greatest figure in modern theology since Schleiermacher, occupying an honored position among the great élite of the church—Augustine, Anselm, Aquinas, Luther, and Calvin.

Karl Barth, born in 1886, began his career as a minister in Geneva, and then continued it in Safenwil, in Aargau Canton. It was there he published the first edition of his celebrated commentary on the Epistle to the Romans [1] (1918), which exploded like a bomb in the religious thought of Europe, and marked the beginning of one of the great eras in the history of Christian thought. Two years later he was called to a chair at the University of Göttingen in Germany. In 1925 he went to the University of Münster, and in

* Thomas F. Torrance is professor of Christian dogmatics at the University of Edinburgh, Scotland, and outstanding interpreter of Barth to the English-speaking world.

1930 he became professor at the University of Bonn, where he lectured to overflowing classrooms until forced to leave under the Nazi régime because he refused to take the oath demanded by Hitler. Called back to Basel in Switzerland, his home, he has remained there ever since.

How Barth's Thought Developed

Three distinct stages mark the development of Barth's thought. In them he wrestled with modern philosophy and then came out with the consistent biblical dogmatics of which he is the master exponent.

I

In his early period Karl Barth's theology falls within the thought-forms represented by Schleiermacher—that is, the liberal theology of religious individualism that developed in the nineteenth century. But Barth's liberalism and idealism were of a strange sort, for even at this period we find searching questions directed to everything before him as the young theologian sought to probe down to the depths. But this ruthless criticism was mainly in the form of self-criticism, for Barth was acutely aware of sin as man's desire to be independent of God. Out of this stage came his commentary on the Epistle to the Romans (1918).

II

The second stage was marked by a radical rewriting of that book. The first edition had not received much notice, but the second edition raised a storm in the theological and philosophical thought of Germany and Switzerland. In it Barth expressed his deep dissatisfaction with the subjectivism of Protestant theology which confounded man with God and put man in the place of God. The new edition was deliberately intended to create an upheaval, and it succeeded. This is the stage of Barth's thought in which he comes under the influence of Kierkegaard, and his searching questions begin to bear some positive fruit. The main theme can be described thus: Let God be God, and let man learn again how to be man, instead of trying to be as God. The supreme sin of man is that even in his religion he is always twisting the truth to suit his own selfish ends and private ideas. Barth is here revealed to be a real genius in theological penetration and expression, for with the most powerful and dramatic strokes of his pen that analysis was driven into all aspects of modern life and thought. His *Romans* translation shattered the selfish individualism of theological liberalism or else made it hysterically angry! But its whole purpose was to make room again for the holy and transcendent God of the Bible.

When man is thus confronted by God, there there is collision, crucifixion. The cross is seen to be the supreme and unique event of the meeting between Holy God and sinful man, and at the cross all the subtle attempts of man at self-deification and self-aggrandizement are exposed. That is particularly true of religious man, for it is primarily religious man who is the sinner. It was, after all, religious man who crucified Jesus! And yet the incredible, breath-taking fact about the cross is the sheer grace and infinite love of God, which tears away from man his rags of self-deceit, and clothes him in the righteousness of God in order to stand him on his feet again as a child of the Heavenly Father.

This is the stage in which Barth's theology is *dialectical* in form. His searching questions have led him to the point where he thinks about the contrasts of Holy God and sinful man, Creator and creature, grace and judgment, God's *Yes* and yet God's *No.* And here Barth is faced with a fundamental problem of all theology and all thinking about God. It is *man* who thinks, *man* who asks searching questions about God, *man* who is hungry to know God, to speak about him and make judgments about him. But when that man stands face to face with God, he discovers that he stands at the bar of God's judgment and it is *God* who speaks to him. *What is important is not what man thinks about God but what God thinks about man!*

This is also the stage when Barth thinks of the relation between God and man in terms of continuing crisis, in which eternity confronts time and God is always invading history and becoming contemporaneous. All meeting with God is thought of as recurring encounter between the divine "Thou" and the human "I". This was Barth's way of answering the problem of communication: how we are to get across to Jesus or let Jesus Christ get across to us without secretly turning him into a twentieth-century figure who is only too harmless and familiar.

The solution for Barth came as a result of tireless criticism of himself and a relentless searching of the Scripture. He let Christ speak to him out of the Bible not as one who could confirm or agree with the theologian's answers but as one who was *against* Barth's own self and against man's desire to make out of Jesus a modern idol.

From now on his theology became the *theology of the Word*. Henceforth the concrete Word of God, speaking to him out of the Holy Scriptures, becomes the object of theological knowledge and security.

III

In the second stage Barth had written the first volume of a new dogmatics, called *Christian Dogmatics*. Now, in his determination to lay the foundations for a consistent and thoroughgoing biblical theology, he found he had to rewrite the whole thing. In the first volume of *Church Dogmatics* (1932), he swept aside all the language of idealist philosophy, all the language of Kierkegaard and the existentialist misunderstanding of Kierkegaard; he threw out the old dialectic between eternity and time and its language of timeless crisis, and interpreted the Word of God in the most concrete terms, strictly in the terms of the Person of Jesus Christ, the Word made flesh, who is true God and true man in one Person.

His Contribution

Barth's arrival at this understanding of Christ is the decisive point in his theological development. We can therefore now turn from tracing his development to describing three of his major contributions to Christian thinking.

The Centrality of Jesus Christ. The great heart of Barth's theology is the doctrine of Jesus Christ. In him who is true God and true man in one person we are confronted with a mystery that is more to be adored than expressed, so that even when we have done all that it is our duty to do in theological understanding and expression, we must confess that we are unprofitable servants of the Word of God, whose efforts fall far short of its incarnate glory. Nevertheless, we must give ourselves to the obedience of Christ, and let all our thinking be taken captive by him. It is only as we become conformable in mind to Christ that we can formulate aright our doctrine of God—Father, Son, and Holy Spirit. That is why the doctrine of the person and work of Christ forms the center and core of all Christian theology and determines all our thinking in the Christian church. And that is why everything depends on faithful obedience to the Scriptures.

It is in this way that Barth himself has already given the church a most valuable account of Christology. For more than a hundred years the theologians and scholars of Europe and America have been seeking to express as fully as possible the truth about Jesus Christ. The documents of the New Testament have been subjected to the most elaborate research the world has ever given them, and how many and how baffling are the problems they have revealed! But in Karl Barth we have another Athanasius, doing battle against misunderstanding on the right and on the left, and out of it all leading the Christian church back to a fuller and far more adequate account of the person and work of Christ than we have known for centuries.

The Doctrine of the Church. Karl Barth's theology has become an ecumenical force not only because it strikes down into the heart of the matter as it affects every church and because it brings within its range the whole history of catholic theology, but also because it has raised into the forefront in unparalleled fashion the doctrine of the church. That was not his deliberate intention. His intention has always been to clear away the ground and to confront the church with Jesus Christ in all his majesty and grace. But in doing this he has forced upon our generation a reconsideration of the doctrine of the church as the body of Christ, and a reconsideration of the whole procedure of theology as the discipline that we must undertake within the bounds of the church where the voice of Christ is heard in the preaching of the gospel and where Christ makes us able to participate in his life, death, and resurrection by his Spirit through Word and sacraments.

In this Karl Barth follows above all in the tradition of John Calvin, though he has brought his searching questions to bear on the teaching of Calvin as well, with great benefit in a remarkable clarification of the doctrine of election.

The New Creature in Christ. In some ways the most characteristic aspect of Barth's theology is his emphasis upon the new humanity in Jesus Christ, incarnate, crucified, and risen, and who will come again to renew the heaven and the earth. This is particularly characteristic, because here Barth's thought moves, as elsewhere, in what he calls a "third dimension." By that he means that whereas many theologians in Europe and America think primarily in terms of two dimensions, God and man, eternity and time, Barth's thinking is governed by the dimension of the union of God and man in Christ. Thus he thinks not in terms of man but in terms of the new humanity that mankind has in Jesus Christ risen from the dead. That is Barth's Christian humanism, and it is that which lies behind his consuming interest in the everyday affairs of our human life and work, social and political as well as religious. (This interest is seen best in his essays published under the title *Against the Stream,* noted under "For Further Reading.")

The central issue here is in many ways the doctrine of the resurrection of Jesus Christ in body. If Jesus

Christ is risen only in spirit—whatever that means!—then he is, so to speak, but a ghost with no relevance to men and women of flesh and blood in history. If Jesus Christ exists no longer as man, only at the right hand of the Father, then we have little ground for hope in this life. It is the risen humanity of Christ that forms the very center of the Christian's hope, for this is the ground and basis of the Christian's own renewal of all creation. The Christian church that believes in the resurrection of Jesus Christ from the dead has no right to despair of "this weary world of ours" or to be afraid of its utter dissolution into nothing. Jesus Christ is risen from the dead and completely victorious over all the mighty demonic forces of destruction that threaten our world. In him we can lift up our heads and laugh in face of fear and disaster, for in him we are more than conquerors over all, knowing that God, who raised up Jesus Christ from the dead, wearing our humanity, will not suffer the world for which Christ died and rose to see corruption.

The doctrine of the new humanity in Christ is the new wine that bursts the old bottles. It is because the Christian church participates already through the Spirit in the risen Jesus that the Christian church must refuse to live in the graveclothes of the past; it must ever be seeking to work out in the present the appropriate forms of its new life in Christ. That is the realism that lies behind the evangelization of the world and the Christian insistence that from day to day in every sphere of our world we must live out the new life which we are given by the Saviour of men.

FOR FURTHER READING

Karl Barth, *Dogmatics in Outline* (Philosophical Library, 1949). Read this book to see Barth's comprehensive theology in brief scope.

———, *Prayer* (Philadelphia: Westminster Press, 1952) and—

———, *Against the Stream* (Philosophical Library, 1954). These two books are brief and readable on certain subjects.

VI

EMIL BRUNNER

BY HUGH T. KERR*

The old German-speaking Swiss city of Zurich, where Zwingli introduced the Protestant Reformation 450 years ago, is today inevitably associated with the name of Emil Brunner. If Zwingli's contribution to Reformation theology was eclipsed by the more prophetic and systematic emphases of Luther and Calvin, so too it may be that Brunner's theological significance has been partially overshadowed by the more aggressive and radical emphases of Kierkegaard and Barth.

Zwingli's indebtedness to Calvin and his personal and theological misunderstanding with Luther are not unlike Brunner's affinity for Kierkegaard and his vigorous running debate with Barth. But if Zwingli's contribution to sixteenth-century Reformation theology was both constructive and substantial, as it certainly

* Hugh T. Kerr is professor and chairman of the department of systematic theology, Princeton Theological Seminary, and editor of the quarterly *Theology Today*.

was, Brunner's theology in our day deserves to stand on its own feet and not be dismissed, as is sometimes done, as a mere disgruntled echo of Barth. As a matter of fact, just as Zwingli's more conciliatory views (on the Lord's Supper, for example) have had enormous currency within Protestantism, so Brunner has been more widely read and studied, especially in America, than either Kierkegaard or Barth.

American religious thinkers tend to be suspicious of schools of theology from the continent of Europe which seem to them one-sided and provincial, and perhaps unduly pessimistic in their orientation. The American traditions are mixed and variegated, and American religious life and thought invariably acquires functional and pragmatic accents. An American Protestant can understand Kierkegaard's ruthless and shattering attack upon the Lutheran State Church of Denmark with its conventional morality and complacent orthodoxy; he can grasp something of Barth's unyielding insistence upon a theology of the Word of God which will have no truck with philosophy or science or with what the common man is thinking. But Brunner, many would feel, speaks more directly to the human situation, partly because he is more cosmopolitan, partly because he is more eager to relate theology to man's present problems, and partly because his books have been more readily translated and circulated in the English-speaking world.

Though he has lived most of his life in his native Zurich, where he was born on December 23, 1889, Brunner—unlike Barth, who prefers to stay put—has always been going places. He studied in New York as well as in Zurich and Berlin, was a pastor in a Swiss village, and has taught in the United States. In 1953 he went to the newly organized International Christian University in Tokyo, Japan, where for reasons of health he retired after two years to return to his beloved Zurich.

Brunner is usually classified as a crisis, neo-orthodox, or dialectical theologian, and this serves to relate him with the others to whom these labels are applied: Kierkegaard, Barth, Niebuhr, Tillich, Bultmann, and others. But like all these, Brunner does not stay put in any pigeonhole or category. Very conservative, fundamentalistic thinkers feel that he is too radical, especially in his view of the Bible and revelation. More liberal thinkers, on the other hand, are convinced that he is too reactionary and that he has capitulated to a restraining biblicism and dogmatism. What one makes of Brunner depends much upon where one stands to begin with. But this kind of name calling and label fixing serves very little useful purpose; more important is it to know how Brunner understands his own theological task and responsibility, and how his many books and articles reflect his interpretation of the significance of the Christian gospel for our day.

A Missionary Theology

To begin with, it is instructive to note how *systematic* and *comprehensive* Brunner has been in his pursuit of an articulate and vertebrate Christian theology. Some of his books were general and interpretative; but since the publication of his doctrinal study of Christ, *The Mediator,*[1] 1927, Brunner has been occupied with examining and reinterpreting the major doctrines of the Christian faith. From Christology he moved on to the subject of Christian ethics, in *The Divine Imperative,*[2] 1932, and then to the doctrine of man, in *Man in Revolt,*[3] 1937. A year later he developed in *The Divine-Human Encounter* an important aspect of his theological point of viewing; and, since much of the controversy over the neo-orthodox position centered around the new view of the Bible, he wrote a big book on *Revelation and Reason,*[4] 1941. More recently, he began to systematize what he had already done and to add to it by projecting a three-volume systematic theology under the title of *Dogmatics.* Two volumes have already appeared

(*The Christian Doctrine of God,*[5] 1946, and *The Christian Doctrine of Creation and Redemption,*[6] 1949), and part of the third was anticipated by the publication of his eschatology, *Eternal Hope,*[7] in 1954.

What is it that Brunner has been doing in all this theological and literary productivity? A key to his point of view may be located in a phase which he himself uses—*missionary theology.* A theology which is missionary in both intent and content is one that deliberately combines Christian dogmatics or church theology and the more specialized concern of what is sometimes called "apologetics," or, as Brunner prefers, "eristics." "Apologetics" has to do with the interpretation and proclamation of the classic Christian faith as found in the biblical revelation and the great creeds of the church, and this is of immediate importance for the church and for Christians; "eristics," presupposing and building upon this, must go a step farther in seeking to relate and apply the church's message to the issues and questions of modern man who may or may not be disposed to accept the basic emphases of the Christian gospel. "As dogmatics is necessarily deductive, missionary theology is equally necessarily inductive. Dogmatics says: This is the revealed truth, and this is the salvation of humanity. Missionary theology says: This is the need and the danger of man—and from this the gospel of Jesus Christ is the means of rescue. . . . Missionary theology is, so to say, pastoral work in the form of reflection, just as dogmatics is witness in the form of reflection." [8]

It is at this point that Brunner found himself at odds with Barth, with whom on so many other matters he was in deep accord. Barth, he felt, was a mighty and unparalleled exponent of church theology, but woefully deficient and blind to the task of making theology relevant for man's situation. Not one to keep silent on such an issue, Brunner provoked Barth into an exchange of papers on the subject which at the time generated more sparks than light and seems now to have been largely an unedifying spectacle of theological fireworks.

The issue was, of course, a real one, and Brunner has consistently and steadfastly maintained ever since the need for a missionary theology which would both affirm the church's faith and at the same time engage in conversation with modern man in his own perplexities and problems. In this, Brunner is obviously akin to Tillich and Bultmann, though critical of both on other grounds, but Barth, almost singlehanded, has continued to plow the straight, and perhaps narrow, furrow to which he long ago set himself. This is also perhaps one reason, rightly or wrongly, that American theologians tend to listen to Brunner rather than Barth, and why many throughout the Christian world were thrilled when Brunner pulled up his deeply driven Zurich stakes and migrated to Japan.

In the Reformed Tradition

There are other important trademarks of Brunner's theology which must be mentioned if not developed at length. For example, Brunner is a self-conscious *Reformation and Reformed* theologian. This is Protestant theology in the great tradition, not simply because it takes issue with much in Romanism, but because it accents the positive insights of the Reformation regarding Scripture as the Word of God, the centrality of Christ, the sovereignty of God, the sin of man, and justification by faith. Because Brunner sees the Reformation as the dividing line in the history of the church, he is deeply critical of the post-Reformation theology of the seventeenth and eighteenth centuries which formalized the theology of the Reformers and stereotyped their creative dynamic. This is the period of Protestant orthodoxy; and, in Brunner's view, it has produced nothing but confusion and misunderstanding. Hence his passion is to revitalize for our day the original emphases of the Reformation of the sixteenth century. For the same reason, he is equally critical of nineteenth-century Protestant liberalism which watered down the Reformation theology by obscuring the uniqueness of the Christian gospel. Brunner is, therefore, also a Reformed theologian in the sense that the church and its theology must always be in the process of reformation under the judgment of the Scriptures as the Word of God. Theology can never be fixed in a final form but must be re-formed for every generation.

The biblical revelation, which is the norm and content of theology, is, however, no anthology of religious propositions but the self-disclosure of God in the *person of Jesus Christ.* Thus Christology, or the doctrine of Christ, becomes the central pivot around which and by means of which all other doctrines are to be understood and interpreted. This was the thesis of Brunner's first big book, the title of which expresses his conviction about Christ—*The Mediator.*[9] More recently in his *Dogmatics* the Christocentric approach is developed even more thoroughly. Thus, the doctrines of revelation, God, creation, man, sin, salvation, election, the church, and the Christian hope are all examined from the central conviction that God was in Christ—that *he* is what God has to say to us.

It would be foolish to suggest that Brunner has

solved all our theological problems, or that his system is above criticism or correction. He would certainly not claim so much himself. On some matters he has raised more questions than answers. Striving for a robust structure of Christian thought, he has not always been so systematic as we could wish. Pressing the centrality of Christ for theology, he sometimes ignores or forgets his own presuppositions and is led into inconsistencies. Deeply convinced of the rightness of his approach, he frequently belittles other possibilities and unwittingly presumes that his is the only right way.

But Brunner's contribution to contemporary theology weighs heavily on the positive and constructive side, and a whole generation of his students and those who have learned from his writings are today carrying his theology forward into tomorrow.

FOR FURTHER READING

Emil Brunner, *Our Faith* (New York: Charles Scribner's Sons, 1936). A brief but provocative discussion of Christian beliefs, prepared as a series of talks to an adult study class.

———, *The Great Invitation* (Philadelphia: Westminster Press, 1955). An excellent collection of Brunner's sermons, illustrating how he translates systematic theology into practical or pastoral theology.

VII

REINHOLD NIEBUHR

BY CLAUDE WELCH*

"Moral man and immoral society"—this striking phrase is the title of a book published in 1932 by a man whose name has become a household word in American Protestantism—Reinhold Niebuhr. This was a striking book, even shocking to some, for in it Niebuhr laid siege to many of the most confidently held dogmas of the early twentieth century. Looking back, we can see that *Moral Man and Immoral Society*[1] not only brought its author into prominence, but also was the sign and foretaste of profound change in the mood and pattern of Protestant thinking in the United States.

The spirit of America in the 1920's was one of

* Claude Welch is associate professor of theology, Yale Divinity School, and co-author of the book *Protestant Christianity*.

confidence and optimism. Even World War I and the early years of the great depression had not shaken the conviction that our social problems were approaching solution. This temper found expression in the churches in the movement called the "social gospel." Many of the leaders were sure that all of men's social relations were in fact being brought progressively under the law of Christ.

In *Moral Man and Immoral Society,* Reinhold Niebuhr erupted in violent protest against these easy assumptions. Analyzing the problems of individual and social morality, he saw that the beliefs in inevitable progress through growing good will and social education were illusions, both dangerous and contrary to the gospel. What can be achieved in individual righteousness may be quite impossible for society. Social decisions are never so clear-cut as decisions about personal morality; they are always, to use a favorite word of Niebuhr, ambiguous. We never have a clean choice between pure truth and pure error, good and evil. In man-to-man relationships, in small groups, we can often achieve a high level of morality, of unselfish love; but in large societies, in the conflicts between groups in society, the moral problem is different. Relations are impersonal; men are not related to each other in face-to-face contact, but as representatives of groups with interests to be served. There is not only the self-centeredness of individuals, but there is also the egoism of races, of corporations, and of nations. And this egoism is not restrained and checked by conscience and good will and reasonableness, for our social responsibilities are confused, and our reasoning is unwittingly distorted by the interests of the groups to which we belong.

Thus, Niebuhr comments, "individuals are never as immoral as the social situations in which they are involved and which they symbolize." There is an impersonal and brutal character about the behavior of all human "collectives," with their self-interest and group egoism, which makes social conflict inevitable. Appeals to conscience, efforts of moral persuasion, which may be quite effective in man-to-man relationships, are simply inadequate to resolve social conflict. "Love" is not sufficient for the restraint of evil. Unselfishness is properly the highest ideal for individuals, but the highest moral ideal for society seems to be justice, maintained even by force. Hence the paradox: moral man—immoral society.

A Detroit Pastor

The vigor of Reinhold Niebuhr's challenge to complacency and optimism did not come from mere academic interest in another theory of human conduct. Much came from the experience of a pastor who was confronted in the lives of his congregation with the brutal realities of social distress. Born in Missouri in 1892, he studied at Elmhurst College, Eden Theological Seminary, and Yale University. In 1915 he became pastor of the Bethel Evangelical Church in Detroit, ministering to a congregation of workers in the automobile industry. Here the theme later to be developed in *Moral Man and Immoral Society* was learned in pastoral experience. He describes this ministry in an autobiographical essay in the recent book, *Reinhold Niebuhr: His Religious, Social, and Political Thought.*[2]

In 1928 he left Detroit to teach in the field of social ethics at Union Theological Seminary, New York City, where he still serves.

We have seen how Niebuhr was sharply critical of the optimism of the 1920's (especially among the religious and idealistic) regarding social progress. He was not rejecting the moral earnestness, or the demand of the social gospel that all life, including social structures, be brought under the reign of Christ. Far from it! Rather, he was puncturing the illusions and the self-deceptions that nullified effective social action. He was calling for a realistic recognition of the depth and complexity of social evil, and of the possibilities for effective transformation, thus for an adequate strategy of attack.

As Niebuhr sees the problem, the Christian is always in a paradoxical position. He must face without flinching the reality and complexity of social evil. Yet "realism" is not enough. Meaning for life has to be gained from insight into a principle or ideal that lies outside the situation. We must always insist on the relevance of the Christian ethical ideal to just these social situations—to industrial Detroit, to international relations, to race and class conflicts. The Christian is bound by the law of love, though the law of love can never be purely embodied in social life.

The "Impossible Possibility"

This problem has been even more sharply defined in *An Interpretation of Christian Ethics*,[3] in which Niebuhr speaks of love as the "impossible possibility" and of "the relevance of an impossible ethical ideal." The Christian must act in the light of both the law of love and the genuine possibilities for action. There is no society in which the law of love can work perfectly; yet the law of love provides our motive and standard for action. Only in the light of the law of love can sin be seen for what it is, and only in this light can relative achievements of justice be judged.

The Christian cannot despair or become complacent, lying down in the face of tyranny and social injustice. Nor can he deceive himself with the illusion that some program or other will provide a permanent solution to men's problems. Every action, every social program, will be a compromise. It will be only an approximation of justice, a choice between available alternatives in the light of the law of love.

From this understanding of our ethical situation, we can turn to two other themes that have been of great interest to Niebuhr: the meaning of history, and the nature of man and his sin.

The Meaning of History

Niebuhr has discussed at length the meaning of history in the second volume of *The Nature and Destiny of Man,* in *Faith and History, The Irony of American History,* and in *The Self and the Dramas of History.*[4] The meaning of history is revealed in Christ. He is the "center" of history, the disclosure of God's rule in history, and the meaning of God's love. In him God reveals his law of love and manifests his power to be gracious to men. In Christ new resources of love, wisdom, and power are made available to men. Yet life in history is never fulfilled. Christ comes in judgment as well as in promise. No social order or proposal for reform can be simply identified with the will of God. No human achievement is ever free from the limitations of human finitude or the temptations of self-justification and rationalism. Every idealism and scheme for the solution of humanity's ills is subject to transformation into an instrument of power over others. Much indeed may be achieved, but every creative achievement brings new possibilities of injustice.

Therefore, history always awaits fulfillment in the kingdom of God, which stands "beyond history." The Kingdom is disclosed in Christ, and he is the judge. In him the law is seen to be the ultimate law of the universe. The Kingdom is the symbol referring to God's purpose for the whole of history, to the full "rule" of God, to an ultimate fulfillment and judgment of individual and social life. Within human history we can have only partial realizations of God's will; thus the Kingdom is "at the end of history," or "beyond history." Yet every partial achievement finds its meaning in the fullness of the Kingdom. In every decision men are confronted with the claim of God's rule. Thus the Christian lives both in response to God's rule now and in the hope of the final victory over evil.

Man and His Sin

For Niebuhr, a true view of the ethical situation of man must be grounded in the Christian understanding of human nature. Niebuhr's discussion of this theme in the first part of *The Nature and Destiny of Man* is perhaps his greatest contribution to recent thought. To many, his analysis there of man's responsibility and sin seems the most original and creative treatment of the matter in all modern theological literature.

Many people suppose that Niebuhr speaks of man simply as sinner. Nothing could be farther from the truth. On the contrary, Christianity for Niebuhr has a very "high estimate of human stature," for man is created in the image of God and is responsible to him. Christianity does, however, have a "low estimate of human virtue," for it recognizes that sin is universal —that is, when they are seen in the light of Jesus Christ, all men are judged to be sinners. It is important then to see how sin arises and the forms that it takes.

One must begin by seeing that man is a peculiar creature, both bound and free. He is part of nature and bound by natural processes; yet he rises above nature as a creature of reason, morality, and spirit. He is finite, limited, yet he is free, conscious of his limitations, and able to transcend mechanical or biological determination. And just this is the root of the difficulty. For man, knowing his limitation and his freedom, is inevitably concerned ("anxious") about himself.

Anxiety (in this special sense) comes with freedom; it is part of man's created existence. Anxiety is not sin. It makes possible *both* sin and faith. In his precarious situation, confronted with his limitation and his freedom, man may accept himself in his dependence upon God—this is faith. Or, man may deny his true creaturehood—this is sin, and Christian faith affirms that all men fall into sin. Sin is not just "wrong acts"; it is a distortion that comes at the center of the self. Sin is not necessary (man is not forced into sin), but it is universal.

Niebuhr suggests that sin may take two basic forms. Man may try to deny his freedom and responsibility, and retreat into simple animal nature. This form of sin is "sensuality." (It does not mean that the body is evil; the body is good, and the sin here is an act of freedom and spirit.) Or, man may seek to deny his limitations and to assert his independence. This is the sin of pride, which is the most basic and universal. It is, Niebuhr holds, the root of all sin. This is the opposite of faith, for it places ultimate trust in something less than God.

Niebuhr has explored the manifold forms of the sin of pride with uncommon insight and precision. His concern for realism in Christian action is intimately bound up with his awareness of the subtle forms that pride takes in its assertion of the self. There is the pride of power, of those who imagine themselves completely master of their own existence and destiny. There is the frantic will-to-power, which seeks final security in dominating others. There is the pride of intellect, or moral or spiritual pride, which thinks its own conceptions and ideals free from all taint of self-interest, and thereby assumes for itself divine authority.

For Niebuhr, the Christian doctrines of man and sin are not merely theoretical or abstract notions. They are indispensable tools for the understanding of every human situation. They are just as relevant for the social analyst and the political planner as for the theologian.

The same thing may be said about the doctrine of justification by faith, a theme that runs through all Niebuhr's concerns and brings them together. As we are all bound up in the manifold forms of sin, as our history finds fulfillment only in the kingdom of God, and as our efforts at justice and righteousness always involve compromise and only relative expression of the law of love—so we are justified not by our works but only as in faith we trust in the graciousness of God. Accepting his forgiveness in our confused and ambiguous situation, we have both hope and energy for our striving in the service of God.

FOR FURTHER READING

Reinhold Niebuhr, *An Interpretation of Christian Ethics* (New York: Harper & Brothers, 1935).

———, *The Children of Light and the Children of Darkness* (New York: Charles Scribner's Sons, 1944).

Charles W. Kegley and Robert W. Bretall, eds., *Reinhold Niebuhr: His Religious, Social, and Political Thought* (New York: The Macmillan Company, 1956).

D. B. Robertson, ed., *Love and Justice,* Selections from the Shorter Writings of Reinhold Niebuhr (Philadelphia: Westminster Press, 1957).

Reinhold Niebuhr, *Leaves from the Notebook of a Tamed Cynic* (Doubleday Anchor Book, 1957).

VIII

PAUL TILLICH

BY ROBERT CLYDE JOHNSON*

Christianity always has lived, from the moment of its inception, in conversation with the culture about it. When we look back across the centuries we can trace a zigzag movement in this conversation. There have been eras when the prime concern has been to converse with culture. Theology has utilized the insights and terminology of the cultural pattern to formulate Christian truth, and to communicate it to the generation which has been molded by the cultural complex. In other eras the movement has been in the opposite direction, away from the reigning cultural forms, in the effort to cut the Christian message free from entanglements and accretions which have threatened to

* Robert Clyde Johnson is professor of theology, Western Theological Seminary, Pittsburgh, Pa.

hide or obliterate it. The former movement is called *synthesis* (a bringing together); the latter is called *diastasis* (a cutting apart).

The theology of Paul Tillich is the great monument of synthesis of the twentieth century. There are certain contemporary thinkers, such as Reinhold Niebuhr and the Swedish bishop, Anders Nygren, whose major theological contribution has been of the nature of diastasis. They have labored long and hard to free the message of Christianity from what they feel to be "foreign" elements which it accumulated in the nineteenth and early twentieth centuries. Other theologians, such as Karl Barth and Emil Brunner, have played a dual role, both leading forth in the cutting-apart effort, and then laboring to lay the foundation for a new synthesis. Only Tillich among the major theologians may be fully described as a theologian of synthesis, one whose consuming desire has been to take seriously and utilize positively the cultural needs, patterns, and modes of expression in reformulating and attempting to communicate Christian truth.

THE METHOD OF CORRELATION

Born in Germany in 1886, Paul Tillich came to America in 1933, having been dismissed from his teaching positions and forced to leave Germany because of his anti-Nazi political views. His distinguished teaching in this country now finds him university professor at Harvard, where he lectures both to the undergraduates and to the students of the Harvard Divinity School.

Tillich's drive for synthesis determines the nature of his theological thought and the method which he follows. He calls his method "the method of correlation." In intention it is quite simple, although its basis and implications are deep and far-reaching. It swings upon two contentions: (1) that if theology is to be "saving theology" it must speak to *the situation* of man, his real, throbbing problems of life and death; and (2) that theology and philosophy are inseparable.

It is the first of these two convictions that casts the mood of Kierkegaard and contemporary existentialism over Tillich's thought, and has caused some to refer to his system as "existential theology." He insists that flesh-and-blood human existence, not abstract theory, is the soil which theology must plow. But for him, to speak of existential theology is like speaking of an albino white horse. He even contends that truth is not true—it matters not how well it may be formulated, or how closely it may conform to the Bible and traditional "orthodoxy"—unless it can be received by man, and can speak to his condition.

The structural basis of the method of correlation rests upon a serious trust in the trustworthiness of human reason. Ordinarily when we use the word "reason" we mean simply logical thinking; but by the word Tillich means more than just the process of human thought. He insists that the world is so created that it embodies certain "structures," and that these structures find their intended correspondence in the mind of man. It is when the structures of the mind meet the structures of objective, external reality that knowledge becomes possible. The term "reason," in Tillich's thought, refers to these structures of reality and of the mind, as well as to the thought process.

The technical word which Tillich uses for his assumption of these corresponding structures is *logos,* a Greek term which appears in the prologue of the Gospel of John (where it is translated as "Word"), and which has a long philosophical and theological history. This is the initial point where his entire theology joins hands with classical Greek philosophy.

The word *logos,* in its various forms, can be freely translated as "thought," "pattern of rationality," "reason," or "word." It is the term which is joined with the Greek word for God to make the word "theology." Theology is thinking or reasoning about God. For Tillich, *logos* means reason, understood in the sense of the corresponding structures. It is his assumption of "the universality of the *logos*" which enables him to take human reason with total seriousness, and which lays the foundation for his theological method and system. Human reason, as such, cannot answer the ultimate questions which are raised by the mind of man; but reason can ask the questions, and the answers which are given, through revelation, come to man through this same reason. Thus he insists that question and answer not only may, but must, be correlated, wedded in an inviolable union, with each rooting in the universal *logos*.

The Human Situation

Tillich's theological system is in five parts. Each part consists of an ultimate question arising out of the human situation and developed philosophically, and then of the answer that comes through revelation. He recognizes that the question and the answer interact; but primarily the first half develops the existential "problem," and the last half of the theological "solution."

What does Tillich say about the basic need of man to which Christianity must speak in our day? He insists that "it is not an exaggeration to say that today man experiences his present situation in terms of disruption, conflict, self-destruction, meaningless-ness, and despair in all realms of life." He believes that the various forms of cultural expression offer infallible clues to the way in which man actually experiences his human situation, and thus he draws heavily upon depth psychology, existential philosophy, modern art and poetry, and political and historical fact in his analysis.

Man, he says, knows and feels himself to be confronted by "the threat of nonbeing," or of "not being." He discovers that he is a creature, wholly contingent, dependent upon and ruled by powers—both within and without—which he neither controls nor creates. This poses man's basic problem, which is his *finitude.* He knows the infinite; but he also knows in the same moment that he is not of the infinite. This knowledge comes to him in the form of a threat. Why should he be, and not not be? May he not, at any moment, cease to be? It is this underlying knowledge which forces man to recognize that anxiety is of the essence of his existence. This anxiety is neither temporary nor accidental. It is permanent and universal. This discovery points to his deepest need, a need for "the courage to be."

Why is it necessary to define man's very existence with the word "anxiety"? Man is created free and with unlimited possibilities open before him. "Possibility,"

Tillich says, "is temptation." As man acts, on the basis of the freedom which is the mark of his created nature, he turns away, and separates himself, from God. He does this (1) through self-elevation, as he makes himself his God; (2) through unbelief, as both with his mind and with his actions he denies his intended dependence upon God; and (3) by his unlimited striving, as he uses his potentialities without considering their source or the will of the God who gave them. Man's actual situation, therefore, must be described as one of primal *separation* (the word Tillich uses for the traditional word "sin"). Man has separated himself from the ground of his being, from his Creator, from the One who is intended to be his God.

The results of this separation are disastrous and all-pervasive. It creates a deep loneliness in human life that can never be overcome. It also results in an unavoidable blindness and a paralysis of the will.

In his separated condition man finds that he cannot escape involvement in both personal and collective "lies." He "labels" others, and refuses to look beneath the label. He tends to pervert and destroy everything, making it what from his estranged point of view he wishes it to be. When he is confronted with the necessity for decision, he tries to rid himself of the burden. He dissolves himself in a political movement, or in a social group, to hide his embarrassment in the face of recurring paralysis of the will. This turns him against himself, and against his fellow men. His life becomes competitive rather than co-operative. This produces suffering, which he feels to be senseless suffering. The suspicion of meaninglessness creeps over him. Cynicism and despair, the "sickness unto death" of Kierkegaard, envelop him.

Every effort that man makes to overcome this situation is futile. It only serves to aggravate his condition and increase his separation, because the effort itself is based upon this condition of primal separation. Whenever and wherever man refuses to recognize this, and seeks to conquer his condition with moral striving, religious forms, or social and political programs, he merely inches more closely to the brink of annihilation. The undeniable and unshakable fact is that on the deepest level of his existence man is helpless and hopeless—except where he recognizes this helplessness and hopelessness, and thus seeks "New Being," or quests for "the Christ."

The Divine Answer

Human existence, trapped in this situation, cries out for "a reality of reconciliation and renewal, of creativity, meaning, and hope." This is precisely what is given to us, Tillich says, in "the picture of Jesus as the Christ" which we find in the New Testament. Here is the "new creation" for which we long. "If anyone is in Christ, he is a new creation," says Paul (II Corinthians 5:17). This "new creation" is described by Tillich as *New Being*, the pivotal concept of his entire theology. What we see in "the picture of Jesus as the Christ," he says, is manhood which is not cursed by the separation that disrupts and destroys our lives. He actualized his freedom, just as we do, and lived under all the conditions of our human existence; yet there is in him no trace of self-elevation, unbelief, or disregard of the giver of life and freedom. In his words, in his deeds, and in his suffering, there is an uninterrupted transparency to the ground of being, a continuous giving of himself to God. Here is "God-manhood," the fully human which has completely overcome all separation from "the divine ground."

This New Being, Tillich says, is "the principle of salvation." It is a power that liberates and transforms our separated and torn human existence, so that we participate in the "new creation." Under this power we are united with the ground of being, with God; our inner "split" is overcome, and we are made one again with one another. This is salvation, a healing which is a reunion beyond our separation.

How do we participate in this power of the New Being? Tillich's answer to the ancient question, "What must I do to be saved?" [1] is "Nothing—literally nothing." It is, first and last, a matter of grace. It is only as we are "struck by grace" that the salvation, the healing of our separation and estrangement, becomes possible. This means that "faith" is not in any sense something that we can or may do, but is a *gift* that is given *in spite of* what we have done. We are accepted by God—this is Christianity's message. It is here that we see how seriously Tillich has taken Luther, or how utterly Protestant he is. Nothing is quite so disconcerting to him as the American "activist" mentality, the compulsion to reduce all things to acts and activity. "Sin" and "grace" must each be understood as a "state" ("'sin' should never be used in the plural!" he insists). Sin is the state of separation, and grace is the opposite of sin. "Grace is the reunion of life with life, the reconciliation of the self with itself." This is the New Being which is offered, a "new creation" for us. "It is as though a voice were saying: 'You are accepted. *You are accepted*. . . . Do not try to do anything now; perhaps later you will do much.

Do not seek for anything. *Simply accept the fact that you are accepted!*' "[2] He who hears this voice has been struck by the stroke of grace.

It is thus that the "walls of separation" are broken down. In the knowledge that we are accepted, we can accept ourselves. It then is possible for us to accept one another, without the aggressive bitterness and hostility that have plagued our lives. In so far as we are "in Christ," our estrangement from God, from ourselves, and from one another is overcome in the power of the New Being.

Questions

The theology of Tillich bristles with questions, both for the layman and for the theologian. The most nagging question for the layman is "Can I understand him?" His technical vocabulary is a language which is quite foreign to the rank and file of the church, although his books of sermons, *The Shaking of the Foundations* and *The New Being,* are highly readable and very powerful.

Theologians have raised their most pointed questions about his "theological" use of philosophy, the nonpersonal tincture in his doctrine of God, and the fact that his analysis of man's dilemma seems to suggest that creatureliness is man's basic problem. Serious questions will also be raised about his doctrine of Christ and his interpretation of atonement. And, although his appointed task is philosophical theology, not biblical scholarship or biblical theology, the question remains whether or not he has taken seriously enough the essential Hebraic structure of biblical thought.

There is a wide and serious diversity of reaction to the thought of Tillich in the theological world. One theologian suggests that he is Protestantism's twentieth-century Aquinas; and another equally eminent authority says, "There is no more dangerous theological leader alive than Dr. Tillich." Whatever the verdict of history will be about him, it will include an unhesitant recognition that here is one of those rare and great minds which leave the whole of human civilization in their debt.

FOR FURTHER READING

Paul Tillich, *The Shaking of the Foundations* and *The New Being* (New York: Charles Scribner's Sons, 1948 and 1955, respectively). Sermons.

———, *The Courage to Be* (New Haven, Conn.: Yale University Press, 1952). A book worth trying.
Charles W. Kegley and Robert W. Bretall, eds., *The Theology of Paul Tillich* (New York: The Macmillan Company, 1952).

IX

RUDOLPH BULTMANN

BY CARL MICHALSON*

Rudolf Bultmann, a German New Testament scholar born in 1884, has made a major contribution to Christian thought with what he calls his "existential hermeneutics." All his theological novelties and accents originate here.

"Existential hermeneutics" is a complex label for what everyone does quite normally, and for what theologians must do somewhat studiously. Hermeneutics is the science of interpretation. Anyone who

* Carl Michalson is professor of systematic theology at Drew Theological Seminary, Madison, N. J. Rudolf Bultmann is one of the pioneers in the "form criticism" study of the New Testament; but this chapter deals with his more recent contribution to Protestant thought.

reads books does so with an implicit or explicit principle of interpretation. Whether his reading will be profitable does not depend entirely upon the book he is reading. It depends to a great extent upon how he interprets what he is reading. Hence, even though for Protestants the Bible is in principle the dominant norm of authority for the faith, it can actually have varying degrees of significance, depending upon one's method of reading it.

According to Bultmann, the Bible should be read as any other piece of literature. If this is true, it could save Christians a great deal of trouble. They would not be involved in the endless hassle over the extent to which the Bible is a special kind of book. But how should "any other" book be read? One should enter into its point of view in such a way as to read it from the perspective of the book itself. *One should ask the questions of the book which the book itself is answering.* Therefore, one needs to ask the Bible what it is saying, and not impose upon it some presuppositions of one's own on the subject.

The remarkable thing about reading the Bible from the biblical point of view is that the Bible shows no interest in the facts of past history, or in theological data for their own sake. It rather exposes the life of the reader to the problem of his personal existence and directs him to a solution which rings with the ultimacy of God's own Word.

This suggests why Bultmann calls his principle of interpretation *"existential* hermeneutics." Hermeneutics is called existential simply because the Bible is found to appeal to the same dimensions of depth and self-understanding in men to which existential philosophy appeals. As the American poet, Delmore Schwartz, has put it, existentialism is the philosophy that believes no one can take your bath for you. Martin Heidegger, who was Bultmann's colleague at the University of Marburg for many years and a close collaborator, developed his existential philosophy around the theme that no one can die your death for you. Bultmann takes the position which he believes is held by existentialism because it was first held by Christianity: no one can hold your faith for you.

When a man reads the Bible from the point of view of the Bible and asks the fundamental questions about his own destiny, he hears the Word of God coming from the Bible as a call to complete obedience. His very life or death hangs upon his decision. The authentic response to the call to decision cannot be a body of data which describes what the Bible is saying. It must be a new and meaningful life. When this event takes place, revelation has occurred. Revelation is the event in which God's Word, communicated through the preaching of the church, constitutes one's life as meaningful. The Bible is the preaching in which the primitive church was born. It is the task of the church through the study of the Scriptures, through theology, and through preaching to let God's Word animate the church again.

Preachers have the easiest time doing this. Proclamation begets proclamation in their hands. Theologians and New Testament scholars have the hardest time. Biblical scholars tend to shy away from existential hermeneutics. They try to read the Bible from the standpoint of other books rather than from the standpoint of the Bible. They want to go behind the Bible to see what its sources are in climate, language, and religious history. In the very effort, they are in peril of separating themselves, their own meaningful lives, from the interpretative task—a procedure which the Bible itself does not endorse. Theologians, moreover, tend to substitute statements about the nature of revelation for the preaching in which the revelation comes to life. They talk about the Christ who is God's Word for us as if he were something in himself. Whereas, according to Bultmann, revelation is Jesus as the Word of God, the holy event of God for us, the event that makes our lives meaningful through this act of God.

The Structure Behind Bultmann's Method of Interpretation

Bultmann takes his method of interpretation very seriously, and structures it with the help of certain philosophical ideas derived from existentialism.

The first idea coming out of existentialism has to do with *the intentional nature of consciousness.* Every act of consciousness is always a *consciousness of* something. Every subjective impression "intends" an objective correlate. However, in acts of understanding, it is the relation of the subject to the object that is investigated. It is then that the question of the existence of the object is bracketed, for it is a secondary consideration. Only the question of its meaning is raised, for the question of meaning is the juncture at which consciousness joins itself to the object contemplated. That relationship *is* the meaning. Meaning does not inhere either in the subject (how I feel) or in the object (what it is), but in the meeting between subject and object (what is meant).

The second rather sophisticated structure behind the Bultmann method is taken from existentialism's concept of time. "Time" for existentialists is divided into the customary categories of past, present, and future. But these do not mean for existentialism precisely what they do for common sense. If they did, the present would be a dimensionless mathematical point on a line separating past and future. As it is, for existentialism the present is the dimension in which a man really lives. It is the realm of one's meaningful life. It is what saves us from simply living in the past. Now the past is not, for existentialism, what it is for common sense. It is not simply that which has decidedly happened, once-for-all. It is a realm of inauthenticity, where no decisiveness, no freedom, no life resides. It is always the "*dead* past." What, then, is the possibility of a man's being saved from the dead past for life in a meaningful present? The future! The future is filled with hope. But because it is future, it is only possible. It is not necessary. Because it is only possible, one must decide about it. He cannot know the future in the same way that he knows what is already past.

Now for Bultmann, the holy event of saving knowledge which comes in God's revelation of his word is always in the future. It is what he calls an "eschatological event." By that he does not mean that the revelation never comes. Rather, it is the event which is always coming. In coming, it saves us from our inauthentic bondage to the dead past by delivering our lives into a meaningful present.

Bultmann's concept of history, which is crucial for an understanding of his position, is tied up with both these points: with his phenomenological theory of consciousness and with his existential view of time. History in modern times no longer means what it once meant for the historians. It does not mean "the facts of the past." As Goethe and Nietzsche established, there are no facts without interpretation. History is event interpreted—meaningful events. In the light of Bultmann's concept of consciousness and time, in what sense is Christianity historical?

Christianity is interpretation in which the holy event of God's revelation in Jesus Christ takes place. That revelation is an "eschatological event." That is, it is primarily future, a possibility to be decided in faith. It constitutes my present as meaningful when I interpret that event in an act of decision, an act of obedience, an act of faith.

Applying the Method

Here the real trouble begins, although it need not be trouble if one understands these methodological backgrounds. Was there an historical Jesus? This question compounds the problems. If by historical is meant a fact of the past, open to the scrutiny of the scientific historians, then Bultmann might say yes. He would hasten to add, however, that the Bible is interested not in the past history of Jesus but in his present Lordship. The key to that is in the fact that the Bible is not scientifically recorded past events. The literary form of the New Testament is evidence of that. It is proclamation of God's saving deed, the preacher's *interpretation* of the event of the past.

Bultmann was one of the pioneers in the development of this understanding of New Testament literature by the "form-history" school. When you read the New Testament you ought not to be interested in the factuality, the objectivity, the past existence of Jesus. If you are, you are not reading the Bible from the standpoint of the Bible. It is not that the objective facts are not there. It is rather that they are "put in parentheses" in order to allow the meaningful relation to "happen." The Bible is not a record of events but an interpretation. When it is preached, that is, reinterpreted, it brings the saving event to life in the present. History in the New Testament sense is not an isolated objective event. It is not even an arena in which persons appropriate truths in eventful meetings. History *is* the meeting.

That is not to say that there is not a great deal of past history in the New Testament. There is. It causes the biblical interpreter or the preacher his greatest problem. For alongside the preaching in the New Testament (the technical name for this preaching is the *kerygma*) is another literary form, the myth (*mythos*). Preaching is a way of speaking about God's holy event so as to allow it to repeat itself in the present. Myth, however, in the sense in which it is used in the study of the history of religions, is a way of speaking of God's acts as if they are scientifically determinable events. But, says Bultmann, God's acts are always "eschatological events," events which are in history as possibilities for the constituting of our lives as meaningful. To talk about these holy acts in terms of their location in world space and in past time is to mythologize them.

Miracle stories, cosmological descriptions about how Jesus was born and how he will return, conjectures about the location of heaven and hell in terms of first-century astronomy, philosophies of history, psychophysical evidences of the resurrection, metaphysical speculation about the nature of God and man—all have myth in them. That is, they all step outside the preaching task of the Christian community where proclamation of saving knowledge is the sole burden and where the decisiveness of faith is the sole response. That is why Bultmann, a Lutheran, strongly influenced by the Pauline message of the New Testament, has been urging the preachers of Germany to "demythologize" the New Testament. (It is for this that he has become best known in recent years.) As Paul and Luther taught, justification is "by faith alone"; and to demythologize keeps one from commending justification on some other basis than faith. The mythologizing tendency of the New Testament tempts one to base his faith on historical facts of the past. A Christian, however, is called to base his faith upon the saving act of God which always comes to us as out of the future with no validation except the act of complete obedience in the decision of faith.

Evaluations

Many scholars believe that Bultmann is wrong to wish to demythologize the New Testament just at a time when poets and other artists have come to take up the New Testament myths as the religiously meaningful symbols for our time. Bultmann, however, does not mean by myth what the literary people do. The New Testament myths are not symbols which unite a man with his deepest meanings. Bultmann holds they are falsifications of meaning inasmuch as they tend to treat as scientific history what is really a revelational event. Though they have the intention of the Christian preaching, they are a device which obstructs and thwarts the radical obedience of faith. They drain off one's attention into the question of factualities and, in the process, defeat the artist's purpose, which is to answer the question about the meaning of life.

A great group of scholars believes that Bultmann represents a rebirth of nineteenth-century liberalism which called the New Testament a mythological document. Stripping away the mythological element, it found nothing of any great significance left. Bultmann, however, does not call for a stripping away of myth. Demythologizing does not mean throwing the myth away. It means *interpreting* the myth. In that sense, demythologizing is simply preaching again the gospel of the New Testament, releasing it from the world of the first century and getting it into the life of the present-day man.

Bultmann's demythologizing project (first published in 1941) was originally addressed to preachers. However, Bultmann believes that the New Testament scholars and theologians have one common task with the preacher: so to interpret the Bible that God's word may be heard today. Therefore, a great storm is rocking the theological world at this moment to determine whether a method which might have some justification for preachers can possibly be carried through by biblical and systematic theologians.

FOR FURTHER READING

Rudolf Bultmann, *Essays,* Philosophical and Theological (New York: The Macmillan Company, 1956).

———, *Primitive Christianity* (Living Age Books, 1956).

X

MARTIN BUBER

BY WALTER E. WIEST*

Emil Brunner, in discussing the relation between "ordinary knowledge" and revelation, says that ordinary knowledge "is always knowledge of an object." Revelation involves "another kind of knowledge —that in which the other confronts me not as an object but as a subject, where he is no longer an 'It' but a "Thou.' "[1]

Statements like this, using the term "Thou" or "I-Thou" to explain what Christians mean by revelation and faith, occur time after time in works by contemporary Protestant theologians and biblical scholars. What they mean can be understood best by reference to the thought of Martin Buber, the distinguished

* Walter E. Wiest is associate professor of theology and philosophy at the Western Theological Seminary, Pittsburgh, Pa.

contemporary Jewish thinker, now resident in Israel, from whose writings this terminology is drawn. Buber has been so effective in reinterpreting for modern men what the Bible says about God, man, and the world that Christian writers have reached into his books and gratefully helped themselves.

In the background of Buber's thinking is a rather unusual form of Jewish faith, called Hasidism, which arose about 1750 in the isolated Jewish communities of Poland. Hasidism ("Hasid" means a holy or pious person) was an expression of a very warm, joyful, religious spirit. God was close and real, his presence felt, both in the close personal ties that bind men in genuine community and in a sense of intimate relation to nature.

At first, Hasidism, with its deep sense of the Divine presence in everything, led Buber into the study of mysticism. Biblical studies later turned his thought in new directions and helped him put in new perspective some other elements in Hasidic Judaism. In the Bible, Buber came to see, God confronts man in an intimate personal relationship in which there is a kind of conversation or "dialogue," a real give-and-take. From this comes a new understanding of faith and of religious truth or knowledge. What I believe or know is, in this sense, what *happens* to me when I meet with and respond to another in the fullness of his being *as a person*. This is precisely what the Bible means, says Buber, by revelation. It is not a set of propositions *about* God and man but a series of encounters *between* God and men. Faith, consequently, is not a matter of saying "yes" with the mind to certain "articles of faith" but a positive response of one's whole being to God who confronts him with a personal demand. The call of faith is not "Believe that certain things are so" but "Choose ye this day whom ye will serve," or "Come, follow me."

This sort of relation, to which Buber gives his famous label "I-Thou," calls for a much different way of looking at things than is customary with us. Usually we consider things for their possible uses and feel we know them best by looking at them objectively and impersonally. This is roughly what scientific knowledge, in its efforts to classify things according to their general characteristics and interpret their behavior by laws of cause and effect, suggests to us. It involves a detached, uncommitted attitude to which Buber applies the term "I-It." We can take this attitude toward people as well as toward sticks and stones. For instance, we can classify man biologically (a thinking, vertebrate animal), pigeonhole him in the social structure (employee, draftee, social security No. 4001-226-

839), or treat him as a means to an end (cheap labor, easy mark, eligible bachelor). Buber recognizes that some degree of impersonal structure is necessary to human culture. His point is that we readily forget the I-Thou underlying I-It relations.

In his much-quoted phrase, "All real living is meeting," Buber asserts the need of men to find fulfillment in I-Thou relations with others. The ideal type of I-Thou relationship might be the best moments of a good marriage, in which each partner gives himself to the other unselfishly and yet finds fuller life in the giving. What happens, happens *between* them, in their relation. No one can sustain such a relation permanently, but it can be constantly renewed. And wherever a true I-Thou encounter occurs, there God is present also, whether recognized consciously or not. In every meeting with a "Thou," we meet "the eternal Thou."

The Dialogue of Faith

There are three respects in which Buber contributes especially to Protestant faith. One is his interpretation of the "prophetic" character of biblical faith. It is all too easy for "I-It" thinking to invade religion itself. It can happen when we indulge in traditional theological language about God (he is infinite, eternal, immutable, omniscient, et cetera). It happens when we reduce faith to ritual and moral law, thinking that when we have attended services and paid our respects to decency we have fulfilled our obligations and can turn to other concerns. It happens when we identify first with acceptance of the letters on the pages of Scripture; Buber has helped us to understand how to take the Bible seriously without forgetting that it is "the letter that killeth, the Spirit that maketh alive."

By contrast, prophetic faith catches up the individual in a vivid, lively "dialogue." There are no formulas to follow, but a constant calling for new decision. God even extends to men the freedom to argue with Him. In his book, *A Prophetic Faith,* Buber describes Jeremiah standing before God "lamenting, complaining to God himself, disputing with Him about justice. . . . Man can speak, he is permitted to speak; if only he truly speaks to God, then there is nothing he may not say ." [2] In relation to God, it is better to be honestly hostile than dishonestly respectful or indifferent: "If there were a devil, it would not be one who decided against God, but one who, in eternity, came to no decision." [3]

His Concept of Community

Buber's second great contribution is in the understanding of human relations. The chief respect in which Buber differs from other "existentialist" thinkers from Kierkegaard to Sartre is that he never runs the risk of leaving the individual isolated. In the shaping of his own destiny, in relation to God, the self is at the same time related to others. Hasidism had a warm feeling for what happens "between man and man" in intimate religious community. Prophetic faith adds a sense of God's claim upon the whole life of a people. Buber says, for instance, that Old Testament injunctions against the oppression of widows, orphans, or "sojourners" are addressed to the whole community of the "people of God." They cannot be a "people" when "the social distance loosens the connections of the members of the people and decomposes their direct contact with one another." God "does not want to rule a crowd, but a community." [4]

Buber sees modern man caught in a dilemma, swinging from a radical individualism (every man for himself) to a radical collectivism (every man for the terrible depersonalizing tendencies of modern society, with its bureaucracies, its technological gadgets, its emphasis on life in the mass. Against these, Buber offers a concept of community based on I-Thou relations. Recognizing another as "Thou" means feeling a responsibility for him. As it is expressed in

Between Man and Man, "A newly-created concrete reality has been laid in our arms; we answer for it . . . a child has clutched your hand, you answer for its touch; a host of men moves about you, you answer for their need." Thus is community created. Community "is the being no longer side by side but *with* another . . . a flowing from I to *Thou.* Community is where community happens."

Buber has tried to apply his thinking in some interesting experiments with community life in the new Israel. Protestants might well remember that a distinctive thing about New Testament Christianity was its expression in a new community love. Men need community; they can be lost in a crowd. Yet Protestant churches are faced with their own problems of bureaucracy, highly geared programs, congregational life which often seems anything but warm, dedicated, and alive. Where should we look for the kind of Christian community that is created when men respond in faith to God's coming in his Word?

In the World of Nature

The third contribution of Buber can be only suggested here. There are difficult passages in which Buber says that, just as one can have I-It relations with persons, he can also have I-Thou relations with impersonal things. This is the continuing "mystical" strain in his thinking which he never wholly lost from Hasidism. What Buber seems to mean is that anything—a tree, a dog—may manifest itself to us as a part of God's creation in which God himself is actively present. This causes us to take things seriously for what they are in themselves, not only for what *use* they may be to us.

Protestant thought has been relatively weak in an understanding of nature and of science. It has tended often to abandon the field to naturalistic or pantheistic philosophies. Buber's I-Thou may open the way to a new interpretation of nature and a new way of relating a Christian view of creation to scientific knowledge. What he suggests is that although scientific knowledge of a tree is good and necessary, after such analysis we still have to put the pieces back together, so to speak, and see the tree again as an entity in its own right. But this occurs in a relation to things that is more like the communion we have with a "Thou" than it is like detached scientific objectivity. The world then appears as a "spiritually responsive universe," in the words of another writer.

This is not to say that trees are persons, or that one will necessarily find God if he is moved by beautiful sunsets. Buber is saying rather that the God whom we know primarily and fundamentally in personal encounter can also be met as "the eternal Thou" throughout all his creation. This may help Protestants to recover something of the sense of the mystery of God's presence in all things which has often been obscured in the emphasis upon individual faith and practical morality.

Buber has always remained faithful to Judaism. Christians cannot claim him in this sense, but it is remarkable how much he can offer us from the perspective of his own Jewish faith. One of the things gained in biblical studies in recent years is a renewed appreciation of the distinctively Hebrew foundations of Christianity. We should be able to appreciate more than ever the truth of the statement that spiritually we in the West are all Semites. With something of Buber's own profound respect for the Christianity he cannot accept, Christians can respond to him in appreciation and gratitude.

FOR FURTHER READING

Will Herberg, ed., *The Writings of Martin Buber* (Meridian Books, 1956). Contains parts of *I and Thou,* Buber's basic work.

Martin Buber, *Between Man and Man* (Boston: Beacon Press, 1956).

NOTES AND DOCUMENTATION BY CHAPTERS

Introduction

1. From *Protestant Christianity* by John Dillenberger and Claude Welch. Copyright 1954, by Charles Scribner's Sons, New York. Used by permission.

I. *Albert Schweitzer*

1. King James Version (KJV).
2. New York: The Macmillan Company, 1948.
3. KJV.
4. Luke 17:21, Revised Standard Version (RSV).
5. New York: The Macmillan Company, 1949.
6. New York: The Macmillan Company, 1949.

II. *Walter Rauschenbusch*

1. From *Christianizing the Social Order,* by Walter Rauschenbusch. Copyright 1912, by The Macmillan Company, New York. Used by permission.

2. From *A Theology for the Social Gospel.* Copyright 1917, by The Macmillan Company, New York. Used by permission.
3. *Ibid.*

III. *William Temple*

1. London: St. Martins, 1934.

V. *Karl Barth*

1. Karl Barth, ed., Bible. Epistle to the Romans. Trans. from the 6th edition by E. C. Hoskyns (London: Oxford University Press, 1933).

VI. *Emil Brunner*

1. H. Emil Brunner, *The Mediator* (Philadelphia: The Westminster Press, 1947). Ed. note: The dates for the Brunner books given in these notes are for the American edition, while those in the text indicate original publication.
2. Brunner, *The Divine Imperative* (Westminster Press, 1943).
3. Brunner, *Man in Revolt* (Westminster Press, 1947).
4. Brunner, *Revelation and Reason* (Westminster Press, 1946).
5. Brunner, *The Christian Doctrine of God* (Westminster Press, 1950).
6. Brunner, *The Christian Doctrine of Creation and Redemption* (Westminster Press, 1952).
7. Brunner, *Eternal Hope* (Westminster Press, 1954).

8. From *The Christian Doctrine of God* by Emil Brunner. Copyright 1950, by W. L. Jenkins, The Westminster Press, Philadelphia. Used by permission.
9. Brunner, *The Mediator* (Westminster Press, 1947).

VII. *Reinhold Niebuhr*

1. New York: Charles Scribner's Sons, 1932.
2. Eds., Kegley and Bretall (New York: The Macmillan Company, 1956).
3. New York: Harper & Brothers, 1935.
4. New York: Charles Scribner's Sons, 1943, 1949, 1952, 1955, respectively.

VIII. *Paul Tillich*

1. Acts 16:30.
2. From *The Shaking of the Foundations,* by Paul Tillich. Copyright 1948, by Charles Scribner's Sons, New York.

X. *Martin Buber*

1. From *Revelation and Reason,* by Emil Brunner. Copyright 1946, by W. L. Jenkins, The Westminster Press, Philadelphia. Used by permission.
2. From *A Prophetic Faith,* by Martin Buber. Copyright 1949, by The Macmillan Company, New York. Used by permission.
3. From *I and Thou,* by Martin Buber. Copyright 1937, by Charles Scribner's Sons, New York). Used by permission.

4. From *A Prophetic Faith,* by Martin Buber. Copyright 1949, by The Macmillan Company, New York. Used by permission.
5. From *Between Man and Man,* by Martin Buber. Copyright 1955, by Beacon Press, Boston, Mass. Used by permission.